PERSONAL AND POLITICAL BALLADS

ARRANGED AND EDITED BY

FRANK MOORE

NEW YORK
GEORGE P PUTNAM
1864

JOHN A. GRAY & GREEN,
PRINTERS, STEREOTYPERS, AND BOOKBINDERS,
Cor. Frankfort and Jacob Sts., N. Y.

NOTE.

This volume contains a selection from the best Political and Personal Ballads that have appeared since the commencement of the present Rebellion. They have been gathered from various sources, Rebel as well as National, and are presented to the reader without note or comment.

F. M.

New-York, June, 1864.

CONTENTS.

LIST OF AUTHORS.

PERSONAL AND POLITICAL BALLADS.

PRAYER-MEETING IN A STORM.*

BY BAYARD TAYLOR.

A GALE came up from the sou'-sou'-west;
'Twas fierce November weather:
But the ship had felt such a storm before,
And her planks still held together.
And thus though the howling tempest showed
No signs of diminution,
The passengers said: "We'll trust the ship,
The staunch old Constitution!"

The captain stood on the quarter-deck—
"The seas," he said, "they batter us:

* See President Buchanan's last Proclamation.

'Twas my watch below in the former gale—
I doubt if we'll weather Hatteras.
The wind on the one side blows me off,
The current sets me shoreward;
I'll just lay to between them both,
And *seem* to be going forward."

"Breakers ahead!" cried the watch on the bow,
"Hard up!" was the first mate's order;
"She feels the ground swell!" the passengers cried,
"And the seas already board her!"
The foresail split in the angry gust,
In the hold the ballast shifted;
And an old tar said: "If Jackson steered,
We shouldn't thus have drifted!"

But the captain cried: "Let go your helm!"
And then he called to the bo'swain:
"Pipe all hands to the quarter-deck,
And we'll save her by devotion!"
The first mate threw his trumpet down;
The old tars cursed together,
To see the good ship helpless roll
At the sport of wind and weather.

The tattered sails are all a-back,
Yards crack and masts are started;

And the captain weeps and says his prayers,
  Till the hull be'midships parted:
But God is on the steersman's side—
  The crew are in revolution;
The wave that washes the captain off
  Will save the Constitution.

New-York, December 18, 1860.

"ALL WE ASK IS TO BE LET ALONE."

BY H. H. BROWNELL.

AS vonce I valked by a dismal svamp,
  There sot an Old Cove in the dark and damp,
And at every body as passed that road
A stick or a stone this Old Cove throwed.
And venever he flung his stick or his stone
He'd set up a song of "Let me alone."

"Let me alone, for I loves to shy
These bits of things at the passers-by—
Let me alone, for I've got your tin
And lots of other traps snugly in—
Let me alone, I'm riggin a boat
To grab votever you've got afloat—

In a veek or so I expects to come
And turn you out of your 'ouse and 'ome—
I'm a quiet Old Cove," says he, with a groan:
"All I axes is—Let me alone."

Just then came along on the self-same vay,
Another Old Cove, and began for to say—
"Let you alone! that's comin' it strong!—
You've *ben* let alone—a darned sight too long—
Of all the sarce that ever I heerd!
Put down that stick! (You well may look
skeered;)
Let go that stone! If you once show fight,
I'll knock you higher than ary kite.
You must hev a lesson to stop your tricks,
And cure you of shying them stones and sticks—
And I'll hev my hardware back and my cash,
And knock your scow into tarnal smash,
And if ever I catches you 'round my ranch,
I'll string you up to the nearest branch.
The best you can do is to go to bed,
And keep a decent tongue in your head;
For I reckon, before you and I are done,
You'll wish you had let honest folks alone."

The Old Cove stopped, and the t'other Old Cove
He sot quite still in his cypress grove,

And he looked at his stick, revolvin' slow
Vether 'twere safe to shy it or no—
And he grumbled on in an injured tone:
"All that I axed vos, *let me alone.*"

THE PILOT THAT WEATHERED THE STORM.

BY RICHARD GAGGIN.

HARK! Hark! from the ocean of life comes a cry
Of danger; see treason's clouds darken the sky—
A ship, fully laden with all that is dear
To the heart of a freeman, is now in despair—
Careens in the tempest—oh! is there not near
Some Pilot to weather the storm.

She bears in her bosom a charter of peace—
'Tis sealed by the blood of the best of our race;
She's liberty's Ark, and she proudly contains
All of hope that to nations benighted remains—
Alas! must she perish before she obtains
A Pilot to weather the storm?

Her captain a traitor—and pirates her crew;
He, faithless to duty—with plunder they flew;

She's nearing the breakers, where billows o'er-
whelm—
Lo! there's to the rescue tried friends of the realm—
Oh! joy to all nations, Abe comes to the helm,
The Pilot to weather the storm.

The tempest still rages—the furies increase—
Night deepens in darkness — his spirit breathes
peace;
Undaunted he stands at the wheel, and shall guide
The vessel triumphant through dangers untried;
While friends of humanity shout him, with pride,
"The Pilot that weathered the storm."

Erie, Pa.

SECESSION LITERATURE.

"I received my first military commission in South-Carolina."
Letter of Mr. Richard Lathers.

"Mr. Lathers is an Irishman."
Correspondent of the Evening Post.

MOURN, swampy groves of New-Rochelle,
And Pine Street, tell thy sad condition;
See Richard's gallant bosom swell
When thinking of his first commission.

His native Irish hills ignored,
  How quick the ties of birth-place vary,
And Carolina claims the sword
  That Lathers drew in Tipperary.

Rise up, O pig-skin parchment! rise
  Before my hazy mental vision,
And dazzle all our Northern eyes
  With doughty Richard's first commission.
Say, was't in Dublin fire brigade,
  Or in the green constabulary,
That first great Lathers flashed his blade,
  And boldly fought for Tipperary?

Choice specimen of Irish brick,
  Blood-red with paint of Carolina,
Come forth and save the Union, Dick,
  Now splitting up like broken china.
In taming rabid Northern crews,
  Be thou our smart Hibernian Rarey;
Employ the sedatives they use
  In Charleston and in Tipperary.

When floats on high the traitor flag,
  And frothy Keitt proclaims the muster,
Your weapon from its scabbard drag,
  And haste to swell the general bluster.

When comes the long predicted fray,
Renew the deeds of Harper's Ferry,
Where heroes talked and ran away,
The way they do in Tipperary.

'Tis sweet to think that when the strength
Of ancient Rome was sadly crackling,
Her threatened liberties at length
Were rescued by a goose's cackling;
So, when oppressed by cruel fate,
Our strongest hearts at last "feel scary,"
A *modern* "Greek" may save the State,
And gild the name of Tipperary.

—*Punch.*

DECEMBER TWENTY-SIXTH, 1910.

A BALLAD OF MAJOR ANDERSON.

BY MRS. J. C. R. DORR.

COME, children, leave your playing, this dark and stormy night,
Shut fast the rattling window-blinds, and make the fire burn bright;

And hear an old man's story, while loud the fierce
winds blow,
Of gallant Major Anderson and fifty years ago.

I was a young man then, boys, but twenty-eight
years old,
And all my comrades knew me for a soldier brave
and bold;
My eye was bright, my step was firm, I measured
six feet two,
And I knew not what it was to shirk when there
was work to do.

We were stationed at Fort Moultrie, in Charleston
harbor, then,
A brave band, though a small one, of scarcely
sixty men;
And day and night we waited for the coming of
the foe,
With noble Major Anderson, just fifty years
ago.

Were they French or English, ask you? Oh!
neither, neither, child!
We were at peace with other lands, and all the
nations smiled

On the Stars and Stripes, wherever they floated, far and free,
And all the foes we had to meet we found this side the sea.

But even between brothers bitter feuds will sometimes rise,
And 'twas the cloud of civil war that darkened in the skies;
I have not time to tell you how the quarrel first began,
Or how it grew, till o'er our land the strife like wildfire ran.

I will not use hard words, my boys, for I am old and gray,
And I've learned it is an easy thing for the best to go astray;
Some wrong there was on either part, I do not doubt at all—
There are two sides to a quarrel, be it great or be it small!

But yet, when South-Carolina laid her sacrilegious hand
On the altar of a Union that belonged to *all* the land;

When she tore our glorious banner down, and trailed it in the dust,
Every patriot's heart and conscience bade him guard the sacred trust.

You scarce believe me, children. Grief and doubt are in your eyes,
Fixed steadily upon me in wonder and surprise;
Don't forget to thank our Father, when to-night you kneel to pray,
That an undivided people rule America to-day.

We were stationed at Fort Moultrie, but about a mile away
The battlements of Sumter stood proudly in the bay;
'Twas by far the best position, as he could not help but know,
Our gallant Major Anderson, just fifty years ago.

Yes, 'twas just after Christmas, fifty years ago to-night;
The sky was calm and cloudless, the moon was large and bright;
At six o'clock the drum beat to call us to parade,
And not a man suspected the plan that had been laid.

But the first thing a soldier learns is that he must
obey,
And that when an order's given he has not a word
to say;
So when told to man the boats, not a question did
we ask,
But silently, yet eagerly, began our hurried
task.

We did a deal of work that night, though our
numbers were but few,
We had all our stores to carry, and our ammu-
nition too;
And the guard-ship—'twas the Nina—set to watch
us in the bay,
Never dreamed what we were doing, though 'twas
almost light as day.

We spiked the guns we left behind, and cut the
flag-staff down—
From its top should float no color if it might not
hold our own—
Then we sailed away for Sumter as fast as we
could go
With our good Major Anderson, just fifty years
ago.

I never can forget, my boys, how the next day, at
noon,
The drums beat and the bands played a stirring
martial tune,
And silently we gathered round the flag-staff
strong and high,
For ever pointing upward to God's temple in the
sky.

Our noble Major Anderson was good as he was
brave,
And he knew without His blessing no banner long
could wave;
So he knelt, with head uncovered, while the chap-
lain read the prayer,
And as the last amen was said, the flag rose high
in air.

Then our loud huzzas rang out, far and widely
o'er the sea,
We shouted for the Stars and Stripes, the standard
of the free!
Every eye was fixed upon it, every heart beat
warm and fast,
As with eager lips we promised to defend it to the
last!

'Twas a sight to be remembered, boys—the chap-
lain with his book,
Our leader humbly kneeling, with his calm, un-
daunted look;
And the officers and men, crushing tears they
would not shed—
And the blue sea all around us, and the blue sky
overhead!

Now go to bed, my children, the old man's story's
told—
Stir up the fire before you go, 'tis bitter, bitter cold,
And I'll tell you more to-morrow night, when loud
the fierce winds blow,
Of gallant Major Anderson and fifty years ago

THE SWORD OF HARRY LEE.

BY JAMES D. M'CABE, JR.

AN aged man, all bowed with years,
Sits by his hearthstone old,
Beside him sits in reverent awe,
A youth all proud and bold.

He listens with rapt eagerness
  The old man's every word,
One aged hand rests on his knee,
  The other grasps a sword.

"My son," the gray-haired patriot said,
  "A precious legacy
I give into your keeping now—
  The sword of Harry Lee!
I wore it through the fatal storm
  That darkened o'er our sky,
When brave men dared for liberty
  To stand, or nobly die!

"We prized our holy liberty,
  We hated tyranny,
We vowed we'd die as brave men die,
  If we could not be free;
We swore eternal vengeance on
  Our foes from o'er the sea,
And night and day we bravely rode,
  With Light-Horse Harry Lee!

"Ah! how we loved our noble chief,
  A hero grand was he;
No craven thought e'er filled the heart
  Of noble Harry Lee.

And where the fight was thickest, boy,
We'd see his bright sword flash;
And the heavens would ring with his shout,
As on the foe he'd dash.

"One day—it all comes back again,
Though I am old and gray—
The battle had raged long and fierce,
For we would not give way—
Our noble leader gave the word,
And on the foe we flew,
Resolved to drive from off the field,
The base-born, hireling crew.

"Our chieftain, at the legion's head,
Rode on exultingly,
When a red-coat vile his musket raised
To murder Harry Lee;
I dashed before the hero bold,
Right in the deadly strife,
And clove the base dog to the earth,
And saved brave Harry's life.

"And when the fearful fight was o'er,
The Major for me sent,
And I was led by Captain Carnes,
That night into his tent.

He grasped my hand right heartily,
  The flush was on his cheek,
And tears stood in his manly eyes,
  His voice was hoarse and weak.

"He thanked me for all I had done—
  I know his every word—
And then he took from round my waist,
  My tried and trusty sword.
He said that I must give it him,
  For it had ne'er been raised,
Save in the cause of liberty—
  With joy I was nigh crazed!

"He gave me his own trusty blade,
  That oft had led the free,
And told me I must wear it for
  The sake of Harry Lee.
Ah! boy, that was a happy night,
  For proud he well might be,
Who e'er deserved such heartfelt praise
From gallant Harry Lee!

"I wore this blade all through the war,
  And when the storm was o'er,
I kept it bright and free from rust,
  As in the days of yore;

And when the clouds came down again
Upon our skies so bright,
I buckled on this blade again,
And wore it through the fight.

"And when the soft, sweet Southern breeze,
From tropic regions far,
Came laden with the clang of arms,
And thrilling notes of war,
I took the old sword from its place,
With tears of honest pride,
And buckled it all fiercely by
Your gallant father's side.

"He bore it manfully and well
In regions far away.
It flashed o'er Palo Alto's plains,
And sunny Monterey.
It never was laid down in shame,
God grant I ne'er may see
One base, foul blot upon the blade
Of dear old Harry Lee!

"Now, boy, I draw this sword again,
Alas! that it must be,
That I must count as foes the sons
Of those who fought with me.

My limbs are old and feeble now,
  And silv'ry is my hair:
I cannot wield this sword, and so
  I give it to your care.

"To-day I saw your noble chief,*
  And ah! I seemed to see,
Erect again before me stand,
  The form of Harry Lee—
That same bright eye, that noble form,
  That bearing light and free;
Ah! yes, he's like his noble sire,
  This son of Harry Lee!

"I'm thankful, boy, he'll lead you on
  To the wild battle-field,
For his father's heart within him beats,
  And never will he yield.
Stand by your Gen'ral to the last,
  Obey his every word,
And yield your life before you dare
  To yield his father's sword.

"Now go, and do your duty, boy,
  You bear no craven's name,

* General Robert E. Lee.

And as you dread your grandsire's curse,
Ne'er sully it with shame.
And I, as long as life shall last,
Within this bosom free,
Will ask God's blessing on you—and
The son of Harry Lee."

Vicksburgh, Mississippi.

A NATIONAL TRIO.

HOLT—SCOTT—ANDERSON.

HOLT.

AN oaken strength has this curt Saxon name,
Befitting well thy puissant manliness of will,
Thou patriot-statesman, whose high deeds shall thrill
Far future as the passing time, when Fame
Shall blazon thee, and thankful millions claim
Kinship with thy brave heart, and eyelids fill
As pulses tremble at the wreckful ill
A staunch soul's hardiment so helped to tame.
Thy stalwart arm, grasping th' unmastered helm
From the vain captain's faithless, faltering hand,
As impious billows gathered black to whelm
In treason's dim abyss our mighty land,

By lordship saved the storm-struck towering realm,
Righting beneath thy swayful true command.

SCOTT.

Winfield thy prophet-parents called thee, Scott;
And now, at climax of delight, they fold
Thee in celestial vision, and behold
Their warrior win his highest field; for not
Canadian laurels 'twas thy youthful lot
To reap victorious, nor thy wreaths of gold
Inwove with Aztec palm, will e'er be rolled
With such sonorous hymn from trumpets hot
With fame's fresh breathing, as thy present deeds,
Baffling the blackest treason ever hatched
In the foul nests where brood the godless greeds,
Its crime foiled by a steadfast eye, that watched
Thy perilled country, and its dread needs
With duteous mastership from ruin snatched.

ANDERSON.

Glad lightning, on his myriad-footed steed,
Sped o'er the land, as happiest angels ride
On blissful errands, and, through the flood tide
Of fiery syllables, thy sudden deed
Poured on the nation's troubled heart such seed
Of power, the flagging pulse leaped in its side,

The eagle soared sunward, again strong-eyed,
Stout men looked each on each with freshened
pride,
And stretched to the utmost admiration's creed
Towards mothers that could bear the like of thee;
Who, 'mid mad shrieks of treason's thwarted brag,
With soldier's grasp and true soul's loyalty,
Outflung with kneeling prayer on Sumter's crag
Freedom's broad shield, terrible on land and sea,
The world's last hope—our war-worn, fulgent flag.

THE FLAG OF FORT SUMTER.

When Major Anderson took possession of Fort Sumter, the whole company assembled and knelt around the flag-staff, while the chaplain offered a prayer previous to the raising of the flag.

THE gray light of dawn o'er the rampart was
stealing—
Where Sumter its stern rocky walls lifted
high—
And spread its chill robe o'er the noble band
kneeling,
All vowing their flag to defend or to die.

The low voice of prayer morning's stillness was
breaking,
As solemnly bowing, a blessing they craved;
Then rose a glad shout, all the echoes awaking,
As proudly unfolding their flag o'er them waved.

Hurrah! for the banner thus boldly left flowing
And flinging its bright stars and stripes to the sky;
Hurrah! for the heroes, no flinching e'er knowing,
Who'll guard it unstained or in death coldly lie.

Dear flag of our country! shall foemen assail ye,
And every bright drop in our hearts fail to burn?
Shall rebels beneath thee e'er beat their reveille,
And we not in triumph their insolence spurn?

By the graves of our fathers, who died in defending
Thy fame, to their deepest affections so dear,
And whose voice from their grass-covered hillocks
ascending,
In eloquent pleadings for thee we now hear;

By the future which stretches in vista before us,
By the echoes which sound from a glorious past,
In purity still shall thy folds yet wave o'er us,
Or drenched in our life-blood enshroud us at last

ABRAHAM LINCOLN — THE MOHAMMED OF THE MODERN HEGIRA.

AT midnight, in the Keystone State,
  Old Abe was *dreaming* of the hour
When Southern rebels, soon or late,
  Should tremble at his power;
In *dreams* "Old Fuss and Feathers" bore
The trophies of a conqueror;
In *dreams* his song of triumph heard,
Then waved the Union banner, stirred
  O'er Southern forts by Southern gales,
And planted down his foot as firm
  As when he split his rails.

An hour passed on—Old Abe awoke
  To sounds that made him pale;
Not triumph this, nor friendly joke—
"*To flight—they wait—by rail—by rail!*"
He woke to list, 'midst sobs and tears,
A tale of horror and of fears—
  And death to be *his* lot—
For lurking near the morning train,
Plug Uglies wait in might and main,
  With dirk and pistol-shot!

"Fly ere the morning's sun arise;
Fly from the foe that waiting lies;
Fly 'neath this *all*-concealing guise,
To Scott and Washington!"
They begged like men inspired by dread,
They told their tale of murder grim—
They conquered—and old Abr'ham fled,
Trembling in every limb.
His *wife* and other comrades watch
The gliding train, his form to catch,
And felt *his* danger past;
But when the morning sun arose,
They dared the rail and all his foes,
Yet *safe* arrived at last!

And thus our hero, by his flight,
Has won the White House on the fourth,
And by *rail-splitting* and his height
Will rule the North with all his might,
Negroes and whites, henceforth.
And learn from this the truth sublime—
"That *he* who runs away,"
Saves life and limb, while gaining time,
"To fight another day."

New-Orleans, March 5, 1861.

—*New-Orleans Crescent.*

KING COTTON.

After Béranger.

BY R. H. STODDARD.

SEE this new king who comes apace,
    And treats us like a conquered race;
He comes from Dixie's Land by rail,
His throne a ragged cotton-bale.
        On to the White House straight
        He's marching—rather late,
        Clanking along the land,
        The shackles in his hand.
            Hats off! hats off!
Ye slaves of curs begotten,
Hats off to great King Cotton!

"White niggers, mudsills, Northern scum,
Base hirelings, hear me, and be dumb;
What makes this country great and free?
'Tis me, I tell you—only me!
        Beware, then, of my might,
        Nor dare dispute my right,
        Or else you'll find, some day,
        There'll be the devil to pay!

Hats off! hats off!
Ye slaves of curs begotten,
Hats off to great King Cotton!

"Dare you dispraise my royal parts,
And prate of Freedom, Commerce, Arts?
What are they to my pedigree?
Why, Adam was an F. F. V.!
My arms (a whip, ye fools,
Above a bloodhound, *gules!*)
Declare my house and birth—
The king of kings on earth!
Hats off! hats off!
Ye slaves of curs begotten,
Hats off to great King Cotton!

"Paupers, who can resist me? None!
My wife's a pew in Washington;
My youngest son—he looks like me—
Will be in Congress soon, (S. C.)
His brother, Colonel Fuss,
Trained by old U. S.,
Tore down your dirty flag—
A General, now with Bragg!
Hats off! hats off!
Ye slaves of curs begotten,
Hats off to great King Cotton!

"Let us alone, ye Federal crew,
Nor dare collect our revenue;
For gentlemen, from earliest date,
Were never useful to the State.
Thanks to my forts, and guns,
And arsenals, (*yours*, once!)
I can now speak my mind,
As ancient Abe shall find!
Hats off! hats off!
Ye slaves of curs begotten,
Hats off to great King Cotton!

"God's ministers, we fight for you;
Aid us, ye aid the Gospel too.
For you, beast-people, (clear the track!)
Still bear our saddles on your back!
We'll ride you all your lives;
Your daughters, too, and wives,
Shall serve us in our need,
And teach our girls to read!
Hats off! hats off!
Ye slaves of curs begotten,
Hats off to great King Cotton!

"Your musket, chaplain—(mind my toes!)
The smoke is incense in my nose!

On then, Confederates, great and small!
Down with the Union—death to all!
From my brave ancestry,
These rights descend to me,
And all true Southern men,
World without end. Amen.
Hats off! hats off!
Ye slaves of curs begotten,
Hats off to great King Cotton!"

May 26, 1861.

THE FAIR AND THE BRAVE.

A FLAG was presented at Bellefonte, Ala., to the "Jackson Hornets," by eleven young ladies, who came forward, and delivered a stanza each, "written by a Tennessee poetess, in the order that the sovereignties left the Union."

MISS MATILDA FENNELL—SOUTH-CAROLINA.

FIRST to rise against oppression,
In this glorious Southern band;
Home of dead and living heroes,
South-Carolina takes her stand!

MISS LUCINDA FRAZIER—FLORIDA.

And I come with greeting, sisters,
Where, amid her orange bowers,

Waves fair Florida her sceptre,
Crowned with rarest, sweetest flowers.

MISS ALICE EATON—GEORGIA.

Lo! and Georgia then uprising,
Burning with the blood of yore,
Sends her children forth to conquer
Peace from haughty foes once more!

MISS KATE FENNELL—ALABAMA.

In the new-born arch of glory,
Lo! where shines the central star,
Alabama, and her radiance
Never cloud of shame shall mar.

MISS CORNIE CAPERTON—MISSISSIPPI.

Sisters! room for Mississippi,
Well she knows the martial strain;
She has marched of old to battle,
She will strike her foes again!

MISS SALLIE SNODGRASS—LOUISIANA.

A voice from Louisiana,
Lo! her brave sons arise,
Armed and ready for the conflict,
Stern defiance in their eyes!

MISS PARTHENIA BRYANT—TEXAS.

Texas, youngest 'mid her sisters,
  Joins her earnest voice to theirs;
Forth she sends her gallant Rangers,
  With her blessings and her prayers.

MISS SALLY FENNELL—VIRGINIA.

Wave, wave on high your banners!
  For the "Old Dominion" comes,
With the lightning comes the thunder,
  Lo! where sound her army's drums!

MISS SALLIE CARTER—ARKANSAS.

Long Arkansas waited, hoping,
  Clinging to the flag of stars;
Now she tears it down forever,
  Ho! away then for the wars!

MISS JENNIE ARMSTRONG—NORTH-CAROLINA.

Over vale and over mountain,
  Pealing forth in triumph high,
Comes a lofty swell of music,
  The "Old North State's" battle cry!

MISS KATE MATTOX—TENNESSEE.

Last, but far from least, among ye,
Spartan band of brave and free;
Like a whirlwind in her anger,
Wheels in line "Old Tennessee."

The "Jackson Hornets" ought to sting the enemy in good fashion, after such a flag presentation.

—*Charleston Mercury.*

A SONG TO ABE.

I.

UP and bear the sway, Abe,
Up and bear the sway;
Let Treason know she has a foe,
And Freedom has a stay, Abe!
You're the pride of all, Abe,
You're the pride of all, Abe,
You're the pride of all the braves
Now ready at your call, Abe.

II.

Up and bear the sway, Abe, etc.,
Thousands sigh and weep, Abe,
Thousands sigh and weep, Abe,

Thousands sigh and weep and cry,
To enter Freedom's Gate, Abe,

III.

Up and bear the sway, Abe, etc.,
Thousands in their might, Abe,
Thousands in their might, Abe,
Will ready march at your command,
And die for Freedom's right, Abe.

IV.

Up and bear the sway, Abe, etc.,
You're the pride of all, Abe,
You're the pride of all, Abe,
E'en traitors yet will bow the knee,
And own your honored call, Abe.

W. B.

A VISION OF JANUARY FOURTH.

BY CATHERINE LEDYARD.

LYING on my couch a night or two ago,
I had a solemn vision of penitential woe;
Of that great time of fasting and of humiliation
Proposed by pious James unto our sinful nation.*

* See Buchanan's Recommendation to the People of the United States, December fourteenth, 1860, published in the REBELLION RECORD, Vol. I.

All the stores were closed the whole length of
Broadway,
As on that great occasion, the Prince's procession
day,
And the solemn chimes of Trinity through the air
began to swim,
Tolling the grand Old Hundred and Luther's Judg-
ment Hymn.

Ah! soon the great procession moved slowly from
the Park;
'Twas headed by the Mayor, and brought up by
men of mark,
Barefooted, marched through mingled mud and
snow,
Girdled with rope, and ashes-strewn, and clad in
weeds of woe.

There were some Republican leaders, feeling very
blue indeed,
That their party, after hard fighting, had the ill
luck to succeed;
They were all for "conciliation," "concession," and
"compromises;"
Hungry to eat their own words and back out of
their own devices.

Houses in Southern trade, although their skirts
were clear,
Had, for the sake of example, come in from far and
near;
They bore a sable banner, all lettered in golden
foil,
"After eating *so much dirt*, are we asked to swallow
free soil?"

Merchants with "woolly" clerks, or those who in
sinful way
Had thought their own thoughts sometimes on the
questions of the day,
Marched with sorrowful tread, in garments as dark
as death,
Beating their breasts, and crying "*Mea culpa*" with
every breath.

There was the British Consul, walking subdued and
meekly;
He had read that statesmanlike paper of Morse in
the recent *Weekly*,
Unmasking the foul designs of the island across the
ocean,
And he hastened to add his mite of penitence and
devotion.

Many were the devices the mournful band upbore,
In token of heartfelt sorrow that would go and sin no more;
Loyal—repentant—humble—and all that sort of thing—
There was one in the style of Blondel—"O Cotton! O our king!"

It was a gloomy progress—no shouts or waving of palms—
They chanted *De Profundis* and the Penitential Psalms,
Or a verse of *Dies Iræ* by way of a little variety,
Tears and groans and ejaculations thrown in to prevent satiety.

Whenever the song was still the bands took up the wail—
(The drums and bugles wore crape as deep as a widow's veil)—
And the players moved along, solemn and slowly all,
To the music of Roslin Castle and the Dead March in Saul.

The route of the procession was up Broadway to
Grace,
Where prayers were to be offered befitting the desperate case;
But a breakfast-bell rang near me, and roused by
its thrilling stroke,
Just on the corner of Tenth street I lost the vision
and woke.

YE FLYGHT OF YE RAYL-SPLITTER.

A BALLAD.

OF all ye flyghts that ever were flown,
By several persons or one alone—
Of science, or Dr. Franklin's kite;
Of "Mincio" Raymond away from the fight,
Or the flight of Professor Lowe's balloon,
From here to England, one day at noon—
The funniest flight of the dreariest bore,
Was Abraham's flight through Baltimore.

Weary and worn like a hunted moose,
Limbs like the wind-mill hanging loose;
Quaking at heart, and flighty at head,
The old Rayl-Splitter he went to bed:

But scarcely in his blankets enveloped was he
When he cried: "I am struck with a bright idee;
Procure me hither, and don't be long,
A hot rum toddy, and make it strong."

Now, various dreams are like to come
From a brimming beaker of good old rum;
And some of them too are just as bad
As any that Tam O'Shanter had.
And so when Abraham laid him down
To dream of doing the Southerners brown,
It chanced that a phantasy bloody and grim,
Came sailing over, and lit on him.

Dead men tossed about like stones—
Broken bridges, blood and bones,
Grinning death's heads, such as grace
Every antique burial-place;
Daggers, pistols, bludgeons, guns,
Thunder showers of red-hot buns
These he saw or seemed to see,
All because of the bright idee.

Then suddenly in from the murky night
There came a messenger wild with fright;

And he cried to Abraham where he lay:
"Get up, old fellow, and hurry away!"
So the dismal phantoms of sleep gave place
To a very practical view of the case;
And the Rayl-Splitter said as he looked at him:
"John,
Just wait till I get my trowsers on."

So he swore an oath by the kingdom come,
That Satan was in that glass of rum;
And he said: "May I never split rails again,
If I don't run off by special train."
Then shrouded closely up to the eyes
With a cloak and Scottish cap likewise,
He left his people dissolved in brine,
And ran away as the clock struck nine.

Swiftly along the Central Road
Went the fiery horse with his precious load,
And at every snort he seemed to say:
"'Tis a Western gentleman running away,
The greatest hegira under the sun,
See if it isn't a glorious run."
Thus honest Abraham, safe and sound,
Stood at last on the Capital ground.

Ah! very noble it seems to be,
This modern standard of chivalry;
And very noble and very grand
Is the chiefest magnate in the land—
Abraham Lincoln, stalwart and tall,
Who ran away, quaking, from nothing at all;
The "honest uncle" in sixty-one,
Who skulked in the night to Washington.

—New-Orleans Crescent.

SANGUINARIA CANADENSIS.

BY JOEL BENTON.

I.

I KNOW the patch where the waxen, milk-white blossoms grow,
On a pea-green palmate leaf by the woody slope of the hill;
Close to the budding coppice, thick as an army of snow,
And the May wind drifts their leaves in a heap by the silver rill.

II.

I plucked a flower from its stem, lustrous and fair to see,

One that had loitered late with a splendor for me to behold;
Saxifrage, Colts-foot, Trillium, Rue, and Anemone,
I bound in a quaint bouquet, with its central nimbus of gold.

III.

Lo! a color of red, of orange, a saffron stain
Darkens my hand, and clings in a multiplied ragged scar;
"What if I had plucked the flower that was planted in pain,
And bathed with scarlet blood my country in crimson war?"

IV.

I thought: "O parricide, traitor, perjurer, villain, knave,
Prince of the rebels, striking at Freedom's consummate flower;
You will carry a damning Macbeth stain to your grave
That shall brighten the name of Arnold to history's latest hour."

—*The Independent, May* 30, 1861.

SONG ON GENERAL SCOTT.

BY N. B. I.

TUNE—*Poor Old Horse, let him die.*

VIRGINIA had a son
  Who gathered up some fame,
He many battles won,
  And thereby won a name;
But now he is growing old,
  And nature doth decay,
Virginia she does scold,
  And all can hear her say,
      Poor old Scott, let him die.

He is old and very mean, sir;
  He is dull and very slow,
And it can now be seen, sir,
  He still does meaner grow;
He is not fit to fight,
  Nor will he ever pray—
Then kick him out of sight,
  And let Virginia say,
      Poor old Scott, let him die.

The sound of his war-whoop
No one again will hear;
In dread laps he his hasty soup,
With hell-fire in his rear;
I had rather be a hog
And wallow in the mud,
Than be old Lincoln's dog,
Or be his warrior stud.
Poor old Scott, let him die.

I had rather be a dog,
And bay the stars and moon;
I had sooner be a frog,
With a dungeon for my doom,
Than to be poor old Scott,
To fill a traitor's grave,
And there in silence rot,
Without a soul to save.
Poor old Scott, let him die.

JEFFERSON D.

BY H. S. CORNWELL.

YOU'RE a traitor convicted, you know very well!
Jefferson D., Jefferson D.!
You thought it a capital thing to rebel,
Jefferson D.!
But there's one thing I'll say:
You'll discover, some day,
When you see a stout cotton cord hang from a tree,
There's an accident happened you didn't foresee,
Jefferson D.!

What shall be found upon history's page?
Jefferson D., Jefferson D.!
When the student explores the republican age!
Jefferson D.!
He will find, as is meet,
That at Judas's feet
You sit in your shame, with the impotent plea,
That you hated the land and the law of the free,
Jefferson D.!

What do you see in your visions at night,
Jefferson D., Jefferson D.?

Does the spectacle furnish you any delight,
Jefferson D.?
Do you feel, in disgrace,
The black cap o'er your face,
While the tremor creeps down from your heart to your knee.
And freedom, insulted, approves the decree,
Jefferson D.?

Oh! long have we pleaded, till pleading is vain,
Jefferson D., Jefferson D.!
Your hands are imbued with the blood of the slain,
Jefferson D.!
And at last, for the right,
We arise in our might,
A people united, resistless, and free,
And declare that rebellion no longer shall be!
Jefferson D.!

HURRAH FOR THE UNION!

BY A. FULKERSON, JR.

HURRAH! for the Union! the hope and the pride
Of millions of hearts that are happy and free;

No shock can destroy and no faction divide
  A work that was destined for ever to be.

'Twas formed by the hands of those patriot sires
  Who fought on the field, in the Cabinet thought;
And not till each vestige of freedom expires
  Shall perish the temple their wisdom has wrought.

Majestic it sprang from the regions of light,
  The marvel of time and the wonder of men;
And, founded in truth and supported in right,
  The blessing still lingers that hallowed it then.

The world shall behold, in its onward career,
  The triumph of reason, the progress of mind;
And man shall arise, and resuming his sphere,
  Leave tyranny, sorrow, and darkness behind.

Go talk of disunion, go murmur "secede;"
  'Tis the dream of a madman, the song of a fool;
For the soul of America laughs at the deed,
  And the star of the Union for ever shall rule.

Hurrah for the Union! the hope and the pride
  Of millions of hearts that are happy and free;
No shock can destroy and no faction divide
  A work that was destined for ever to be.

A SOUTHERN PÆAN.

AIR—*Kitty Tyrrell.*

I'LL sing you a song, worth the singing,
  Of Sumter chivalrously won,
By the brave chiefs who brought to the contest
  Just seventy hundred to one!
Fair odds was the good Saxon usage,
  When men *boasted* of worsting a foe;
But such musty old saws are exploded,
  And we are all heroes, you know.

With such an array, how surprising
  That they had the worst of the game!
Though we poured down our hot shot in torrents,
  Till the fort was enveloped in flame;
With one hand to put out the fire,
  The other might still point a gun,
For, after such stern preparation,
  The work seems too easily done!

The details may well excite wonder,
  Though folks differ about the disgrace;
Had we not stolen Uncle Sam's thunder,
  His flag might still float in its place.

But a Beauregard, Hamilton, Davis,
  Cannot always be had for the call;
Arnold's memory paled in their splendor,
  Until Twiggs flamed forth Phœnix of all.

But a truce to all questions of reason,
  Fort Sumter is gloriously won.
And who cares a jot for the treason,
  If the black-hearted North is undone?
'Tis true this may rouse indignation,
  And parties may possibly jar,
But *we* can defy the whole nation,
  Since we've taken Fort Sumter—hurrah!

But hark! as the news flies to Northward,
  The sound of discussion is hushed,
Each man vowing aid to the vanguard,
  Until treason and traitors are crushed;
From all sides they rush to the struggle,
  One strong pulse is felt through the land;
Twenty millions of freemen and patriots
  United in heart and in hand!

So the song that I deemed worth the singing
  May possibly sound out of time,
And our bells, now for victory ringing,
  Soon slowly and mournfully chime

We may learn more respect for our country,
  And find that, though loudly we crow,
Seven thousand men worsting one hundred
  Does *not* prove them all heroes, you know!

A. E.

THE SPECTRE AT SUMTER.

I STOOD on the walls of Sumter
  As the solemn night came down
On the lone, beleaguered fortress,
  On the traitor camp and town;
While through the lurid heavens
  Sped the red-hot shot and shell,
As if by mad fiends driven
  From the open mouths of hell;
While the flag of a sovereign nation,
  On the palpitating air,
Still waved from its lofty station
  Amid the fiery glare.

And I saw where fiercest, direst,
  Raged the terrible battle-storm—
Where the bursting shells fell hottest,
  There towered a spectral form;

I knew by its proud erectness,
  By its calm, determined mien,
By the strong arms, sternly folded,
  By the deep, clear eye serene,
'Twas that old man, lion-hearted,
  Of the dark and terrible frown,
The Genius of Retribution—
  Old OSAWATOMIE BROWN.

"'Tis well!" he murmured softly,
  "O traitorous, coward band!
Ply your engines fiercer, faster,
  'Gainst the flag of your native land!
Rain your deathful hail more hotly
  On the heads of that faithful few,
Stifled, and faint, and famished,
  With their flag of truce in view!

"Roar louder, ye murderous cannon!
  With every echoing boom
O'er the hills of the sturdy Northland
  Sweeps the story of Sumter's doom
And I hear above your thunder
  The shout of a warrior band,
Waked suddenly from slumber,
  To strike for their native land.

"As the lion of the desert
  Leaps fiercely from his lair,
And gazes down the distance
  With fixed and fiery glare—
As the bolt along the storm-cloud
  Quivers in fierce unrest,
Ere it burst in triple vengeance
  On earth's rent and quivering breast—
E'en so the sons of freedom
  For one dreadful moment stand,
Till your murderous hand uplifted
  Is struck at your native land.

"Strike fiercer, faster, murderers,
  Steeped to the core in sin,
See the flag of your country drooping—
  Aim at it once again!
All Sumter's guns are voiceless,
  And the flames are hot within,
And faint are her brave defenders—
  Aim at her once again!
Ha! dastards, cravens, cowards,
  Ye are brave and knightly men!
Your foes disabled, silenced—
  Fire on them once again!

"Ah! mine is the unsealed vision,
 And mine is the prophet ear;
Ye may laugh in your mad derision,
 But the day of doom is near!
New-England's hills will echo
 With the warrior's battle cry,
And New-York's Excelsior banner
 'Mid shoutings kiss the sky;
From the free North's lakes and rivers,
 O'er the distant prairie's breast,
From true-souled Pennsylvania,
 And the bold, unfettered West—
Like the roar of the mountain torrent,
 Like the shriek of the tempest comes,
'God and our country ever!
 Our banner and our homes!'

"Oh! this is the day I prayed for,
 When against the wintry sky,
With the rope around my throttle
 Ye hung me up to die—
The day when my free-born brothers
 In their lofty faith will rise,
And wipe from their fair escutcheon
 The stain that on it lies—
When Manhood, crushed and blighted,
 Trampled, and bruised, and torn,

And Womanhood, lashed, polluted,
  The victim of lust and scorn,
From their fainting spirits lifted
  The burden and the blight,
May wake from their loathsome serfdom
  To revel in freedom's light.

"My country! O my country!
  I have called on you oft before,
Would God that my strong appealing
  Might enter your souls once more!
As you value the boon of freedom,
  So fearlessly won for you,
Strike home for your firesides bravely,
  And a whole free country too!
Let your proud flag kiss the heavens
  With never a blot or stain;
O'er bleeding human chattels
  Never to float again!"

LA CANADIENNE

BALLAD OF FORT SUMTER.

REBELLION in the sunny South;
  The sound of war again;
A castle in the harbor's mouth,
  With scarce a hundred men!

True is its gallant Anderson;
  Trusty his chosen few;
And loyal every waiting gun
  Guarding the waters blue!

Besieging forces all around;
  Six thousand under arms;
The handful dare to stand their ground,
  And breast the wild alarms!

Patriots on whom fond heavens have smiled,
  Lovers of liberty,
With souls by treason undefiled,
  They serve the loyal free!

For long and dreary months hemmed in,
  A brother's aid denied;
No power life's needed good to win,
  No hope from o'er the tide.

In sight the Star's flag woos the breeze,
  At once death-threatening notes
Come pealing o'er the swelling seas
  From blazing cannon throats!

Dark batteries frown on Sumter's walls;
  Ready the rebel foe!
The heroes meet its humbling calls
  With an unwavering "No!"

Surrender? Never, while they dare
  To call a hope their own;
Blows must be struck for entrance there;
  Might wins—and might alone!

Thus days of weariness pass by,
  Long days of manly toil,
Till Famine sounds its herald cry
  Of victory and spoil!

Ten thousand hearts are with them there!
  Alas! all powerless they!
They can but lift their voice in prayer,
  And fold their hands to pray!

And sturdy ships with precious freight
  Are speeding o'er the sea,

But ere they reach the harbor-gate,
Stern dangers dare the free!

The savage foe with cunning hand
Forewarned of coming aid,
To ruin doom the needy band—
The few but undismayed!

The slowly-burning torch applied,
Quick burst loud thunder peals,
Fire-trailing bombs fly o'er the tide;
The shock proud Sumter feels!

They thicken in the startled air,
As storms of summer hail;
Night reddens with the lurid glare!
Those stout hearts do not quail!

Ere long the gallant Anderson
Returns the heavy fire;
Loud speaks full many a shotted gun,
And death is in their ire!

Most nobly fight the little band,
Beneath the dear old flag!
For that in danger dare to stand,
As deer on beetling crag!

Thus forty hours red cannon throats
  Utter their fiendish cry,
While Sumter with her thunder notes
  Makes resolute reply.

But ah! those brave, how feeble they,
  Before such circling hosts,
However well their part they play,
  Or confident their boasts!

Hot balls upkindle angry flames,
  And stifled grows the air;
The foe still closer press their claims,
  Nor heed their known despair!

Yet no vain murmurs pass their lips,
  When shines no more a star,
Nor succor comes from friendly ships,
  Without the harbor bar!

Calmly they run the white flag up,
  The all now left the brave,
In silence drink the bitter cup,
  From which no arm can save!

If mercy comes not from the foe,
  Kind Heaven deals tenderly,

No dead ones from their presence go,
  No blood-stains scar the free!

The God—the Holy One and Just,
  Who gave them hearts so true;
The God in whom they meekly trust,
  Preserves the gallant few!

While hundreds of the traitor band
  Hear now no signal drum,
From out the rage of fire and brand
  Alive, unharmed they come!

Their hearts are full of filial love,
  For all this guardian care,
But tears will flow to feel, above
  Scarred Sumter, now the fair,

The stainless banner of the free,
  No more shields Freedom's brave
And eager eyes no longer see
  Its triumph from the wave!

To sternest need they only yield;
  Their hearts, unconquered still,
Salute the flag and leave the field
  For Treason's hordes to fill!

But while the world delights to own
  Her few, immortal names,
Shall gallant Anderson's be known
  As one such honor claims!

And millions yet unborn shall hear
  From aged lips the tale,
How those true hearts knew not a fear
  Storming the fiery gale!

FORT SUMTER.

A HEROIC POEM, IN THREE CANTOS

BY CHARLES EDWARD LEVERETT, JR.

CANTO I.

NOW glory be to Uncle Abe, and Scott, his lion pet,
And Seward, the righteous pontifex, who rules the Cabinet;
And glory to the mighty fleet that stood off Charleston Bar,
And left the dauntless Anderson to bear the brunt of war.

The Patriarch in Washington had summoned to his side
His squad of Solons, brilliant men, the rabble's joy and pride,
And some were looking very black, and some were looking blue,
The nation was at loggerheads, and none knew what to do;
And little light had yet been thrown upon the States' affairs,
For Abe, though good at splitting rails, was bad at splitting hairs.
Then up arose that valiant man, Lieutenant-General Scott,
And drew his sword, like Philip's son, and cut the Gordian knot.
"Now, by this waxed moustache," he said, and looked around the group,
"And by these lips that tasted once a 'hasty plate of soup,'
I raise my voice for horrid war, 'tis just the thing for me;
Too long it is since I have had a military spree,
With all our gallant peddlers, our knack at making clocks,
Our taste for wooden nutmegs, and glorious Plymouth Rocks,

Our reverence for a Higher Law, our godly pulpit rant,
With all the talents which in Yankee land are now extant,
A generalissimo, like me, would find it no great thing
To gallop through the South, and whip the Chivalry, by Jing!"
He said, the hero whose chief joy was hearing bullets whiz,
And drew a red bandana forth, and wiped his warlike phiz;
Around the room a stifled buzz of admiration went,
When on his trembling knees arose the doughty President.
"Now, by old Andrew Jackson's shade, and by the oaths he swore,
And by his hickory stick, and by the thunder of his snore,
And by the proud contempt he showed for Carolina gents,
And English grammar," quoth old Abe, "them's jist my sentiments.
Great Seward shall gull the Southrons, like a wily diplomat,
With promises and flummery, with 'tother, this and that;

And I will launch a squadron forth, in secret, on
the seas,
And reïnforce Fort Sumter with 'old horse,'
and bread and cheese;
Poor Doubleday, that wretched man, whose
appetite ne'er fails.
Has been obliged, for three weeks now, to eat
his finger-nails;
While underneath his very nose, the rebels sit
and cram
Their throats with beef, and turtle-soup, and
English peas and lamb.
Ho! then, for Carolina, my veterans, brave and
true,
'Tis high time that the Chivalry should learn a
thing or two;
I swear my hungry soger boys shall soon have
meat and drink,
I, gallant spouse of Mrs. Abe, and Pa of Bobby
Link!"

So spake the "old man eloquent," and hushed
he there and then,
The Cabinet all looked devout, and answered
him Amen.

CANTO II.

Oh! 'twas a fearful thing to see, just at the break of day,
That terrible Armada sailing up through Charleston Bay,
Battalions of Palmetto troops stood marshaled on the strand,
To greet their Yankee cousins, and to welcome them on land;
And banners waved, and tattoos beat, and cannon lined the beach,
All ready to salute, when lo! they anchored—out of reach!

A storm was bursting from the sky—'twas sweeping from the main;
Its clouds were rolling wreaths of smoke, its rain was iron rain,
Its lightning was the lurid bomb, its thunder was the roar
Of mortar and columbiad, bristling on the sandy shore;
A thousand guns were flashing fire, a thousand whistling balls
Were falling in hot showers upon Fort Sumter's blackened walls.

They fought, "the Saucy Seventy," like brave men, long and well,
With wondrous skill and fortitude they dodged the hurtling shell;
Undauntedly they blazed away, with not a single crumb
Of dinner to console them—not one cheering drop of rum;
When, seeing 'twas impossible to fast and fight much more,
They strike their flag, and Foster falls—perspiring at each pore!
Hall waves his gleaming sword, looks proud defiance at his foes,
Then sinks exhausted, bleeding most profusely—at his nose;
And Doubleday, his longing eye fixed on the distant ships,
Collapses, with "My stomach, O my stomach!" on his lips.

CANTO III.

A telegram is flying North, 'tis pithy, sharp, and curt—
"Fort Sumter's taken—tell Old Abe that nobod-y is hurt."

A panic strikes the Cabinet, they wriggle in their chairs,
Seward mutters "curses deep, not loud"—
Welles tries to say his prayers;
Old Uncle Abe, their royal liege, grows pallid at the news,
Uneasy twitch the nimble feet within his nimble shoes,
All downward through his spindle shanks a nervous tremor flows,
And fast the courage oozes from the hero's valiant toes;
His hair begins to stand on end, his eyes are full of dread,
Already in the streets he hears the Southern cohorts tread,
Already through the White House gates he sees the legions pour,
Already dreams their battle-axe is thundering at his door,
Already feels fierce cow-hide boots assail him in the rear,
And finds, alas! the seat of war uncomfortably near!
"Now if," he cries, "my councillors, ye are inclined to flee,

(For 'tis not every one who'd like to face the
Chivalry,)
And if the prospect of a fray should fill you
with alarm,
If ye demand a Captain who will lead you out
of harm,
Pack up your spoils, and while the Gin'ral keeps
the foe at bay,
Put ye your trust in Providence, and set your
legs in play,
And follow where this soger-cloak, all streaming
in my flight,
Is like a streak of lightning seen dissolving from
the sight.
Ho, ho! for Illinois, my braves! hip, hip, hur-
rah! away;
Do what you choose — for me — why, *I'll be
hanged* if I will stay."

Now glory be to Uncle Abe, and Scott, his
bully pet,
And Seward, the cook and bottle-washer of the
Cabinet;
And glory to the mighty fleet that stood off
Charleston Bar,
And left the dauntless Anderson to bear the
brunt of war!

PETER HART:

A BALLAD OF THE SIEGE OF SUMTER.

BY EDWARD S. RAND, JR.

'TWAS when the rebel batteries were firing shot and shell,
When thick round Sumter's battlements the deadly missiles fell,
Where worn and weary from the siege the gallant little band,
Gainst countless and o'erwhelming odds right nobly made their stand.

Then spake our gallant Anderson: "Stand forth, my fearless men,
And give the traitors one more round, and man the guns again;
The flag that floats above our heads was raised with tears and prayer:
God willing, its bright starry folds shall float for ever there."

Then at the word stood forth the men, bold-hearted, brave, and true,
Shame on procrastinating rule, alas! they were too few!

And with a cheering, ringing shout, 'mid shot
and bursting shell,
Right manfully they serve the guns, and do their
duty well.

Yet one remains! say, can it be amid that little
band,
A traitor lurks, to plot and bring woe on his na-
tive land?
Not so! with half-averted eye, tears streaming
down his cheeks,
From quivering lip and faltering tongue, a pat-
riot soul out-speaks:

"Where broad Hudson's swelling tide drives back
the ocean's foam,
In the great city of New-York, I have my little
home;
But chance from all I hold most dear has borne
me far away,
And the same chance has watched my steps and
brought me here to-day.

"But when in Charleston's streets I stood amid
the rebel crew,
They made me swear a solemn oath e'er they
would pass me through,

That come what might, though wrong or right, on water or on land,
Against the Southern foe in fight I'd never lift my hand.

"I took the oath, with faltering tongue, but 'twas to save my life,
And came—it might be I could aid a little in the strife:
I cannot join to man the guns, the solemn oath I spoke,
And Peter Hart thus far in life his promise never broke.

"But on the battlements I'll stand, and call aloud, 'Beware!'
And watch to tell when shot and shell come darting through the air,
That all take warning: Peter Hart must to his oath be true,
But for his country he will dare all that a man may do."

And there upon the battlements through all the siege he stood,
All ready, if it need be, to baptize them with his blood;

And as the rebel port-holes flashed, called loudly, "Shot!" or "Shell!"
And when it struck, then came the word: "Thank God, for all is well!"

Why tell how traitor force prevailed? each child through all the land
Can lisp the story of the siege, tell how the little band,
'Mid blazing barracks, bursting shells, fasting and weak and worn,
Fought till their failing strength gave out, till every means was gone,
And then in honor, with their flag, marched from the stronghold forth,
Leaving the rebels blackened walls, sailed for the loyal North.

O loyal city of New-York! be proud, as well you may,
That yours divide with Anderson the honors of that day;
We loved you as the mighty one, the country's boast and pride,
But a bond now knits us unto you that nothing may divide.

Away with petty rivalry, with every vain dispute,
In the country's song of Freedom, let jarring notes be mute!
New-England sends thee greeting, in love extends her hand,
And we swell the cheers for Union which are echoing through the land.

And not in vain 'gainst Sumter's walls the waves of rebel ire
Broke in a storm of shot and shell, and sheets of smoke and fire;
And not in vain the starry flag bowed to a traitor band;
It has roused to life the spirit of a mighty loyal land.

Already on the eastern hills the dawn of Freedom's day
Tells that the plague-spot of our land shall soon be purged away;
That the down-trodden shall be raised, and ours shall truly be,
As often vainly vaunted, land of the brave and *Free!*

You who have toiled and waited—oh! great will
be your gain.
Ye soldiers in the camp and field, ye labor not
in vain!
Remember each when heavy paths your weary
feet have trod,
To toil in patience, working out the purposes of
God.

Glen Ridge, Mass.

THE RISING OF THE PEOPLE.

BY GEO. W. PUTNAM.

ANXIOUSLY a waiting people held their
stated day of rest,
Quietly the April Sabbath's light died in the distant west,
When skyward looked the watchers, and on their
startled gaze
Fell the light from Sumter's burning walls, and
Northern heavens ablaze!

"FOUL TREASON'S CUP HATH BRIMMED AT LAST!
THE CROWNING DEED IS DONE!"
Thus the lightnings flashed the tidings from the
rise to set of sun!

And then as if the Archangel's trump through
heaven's concave rang,
Eighteen millions from their sleeping to a life
intensest sprang!

Clear in that lurid light stood forth the dark pines
of Vermont,
The men of Hampshire saw its glare on the White
Hills' rampart front;
It pierced Maine's tangled forests, lit the waves of
Aroostook,
And Connecticut's granite boulders with a shud-
dering horror shook!

On country church, on hill-side farm, on city dome
and spire,
On myriad masts, on crowded decks played the
forked tongues of fire;
With the hideous story laden, ocean's waves, a
white-lipped band,
Fell and fainted as they told it to Rhode Island's
shore of sand!

Glaring afar o'er battle-fields, like the red flame of
hell,
Full on the green at Lexington and Bunker's shaft
it fell;

White grew old Massachusetts' face with wrath
beneath that sky,
And through the land her iron heart beat audibly
and high!

The dwellers in Manhattan's isle saw bloody Trea-
son stalk,
Like the deep growl of thunder answered the
voice of York;
As sped up Delaware's broad Bay the sentinel's
alarm—
Doffed her drab the "Quaker City"—bared for
Right her sinewy arm!

All her generous offers spurned and scorned—her
counsels set aside,
The bruised cheek of the North once more glowed
with her ancient pride.
At sight of Freedom bleeding—Peace lost her
wonted charms,
And the cry went sweeping through the land:
"Ho! FREEMEN, NOW TO ARMS!"

New-England answered with a shout! and from
each Vermont glen
The brave "Green Mountain boys" came down
with Hampshire's mounted men!

The white tents of the volunteers stretch inland
from the shore,
And Bunker's Heights and Concord Green are
bivouacs once more!

I read with proudly swelling heart, O "BAY
STATE!"—native mine—
In the fore-front of battle, as in the days lang
syne,
Ere yet the trump had sounded—an angel of the
Free,
Thou stood'st—with one foot on the land, and
one upon the sea!

Maine heard, and from her forest depths, made
answer to the call,
At sunrise Ocean saw her bands pass up her rocky
wall;
While every hill and storm-worn crag waved high
the warlike sign,
Her drums were beating loud "to arms!" adown
the English line!

And from Connecticut's farm-homes her yeomanry
in pride,
With the staunch troops of Rhode Island came
marching side by side!

The vast metropolis in arms, to meet the tyrant
power,
Gave to the cause of justice the noblest of her
dower!

Up northward from Long Island Sound the cry
went hurrying past,
And rolled across the inland seas like ocean's
stormy blast!
Along the Palisades it rang, and up the Mohawk
vale,
And backward came the trumpet's clang and drum-
beat on the gale!

All through the inland counties leaped the electric
fire,
And answered promptly stalwart youth—mid-age—
and hoary sire!
And 'tis said that pointing southward—from where
Elba's martyr lay—
Is seen a flaming hand at night—a shadowy hand
by day!

Horsemen are trooping o'er the hills—wagon-loads
of armèd men
Are hurrying down the country roads from hamlet,
grove, and glen;

Ten thousand country church-bells ring out their
warning peal,
Through the trees the sunshine glances on the
passing Northern steel!

And all in line for marching—on many a village
green,
With loving friends around them, the country
troops are seen,
Hearts are swelling, tears are falling, as the white-
haired pastors pray—
God's blessing on the soldiers ere they go upon
their way!

Westward roll the thrilling tidings—manly voices
high and rough
Shout from the up-bound steamer's deck as she
sweeps beneath the bluff!
While high aloft the "STRIPES *and* STARS" are
proudly waving o'er,
Her warning gun the story tells along the echoing
shore!

Swiftly up the river ravine roads the hurrying
horsemen rush,
Shouting hoarsely as they gallop through the
prairie's softened hush,

To field, to forest sugar-camp, lake-side hut, and
inland town,
On speeds the word two hundred miles ere yet two
suns go down!

Quickly the hunting-shirts are donned, and in the
morning's gray,
With their rifles to their shoulders the men are on
their way!
Matrons, sisters, wives, and sweethearts grouped
around the cabin door,
Wave their blessings on the hunters as they seek
the river shore.

On the hunters who have followed the gray wolf
to his den,
The sons of bright Iowa, and Minnesota's men,
Now to hunt the hideous *human* wolves who make
of man a prey,
With firm-set lip and springing step they hasten on
their way.

Even where Starvation's spectre, like midnight
made the dawn,
Where the tottering forms are many, and the faces
pale and wan,

Long bruised and suffering Kansas—once crushed
'neath slavery's ban,
Claims for her eager riflemen the front of Freedom's van.

Wisconsin at the summons gave up her chosen
ones,
And Illinois sent forth with joy the noblest of her
sons,
And when with silent drums the troops came
marching Alton by,
They heard the voice of Lovejoy's blood still calling to the sky.

Ohio from her thousand vales—Indiana from her
plains,
Send forth their hosts to met the foe up from the
land of chains;
They troop from all the lake-side homes of distant
Michigan,
From Jersey's fields and Delaware who kept her
faith with Man.

Down from the Alleghany range they rush like
mountain streams!
And where they move the earth grows light beneath their pennon's beams;

Their thunder shout for Freedom answers the old bell's call,
That rang her birth-peal years ago o'er "Independence Hall."

In the cities, merchant princes rain down a golden shower,
And Beauty comes as ever to await the final hour;
All day the nimble fingers sew—all night beside the lamp,
And woman's voice and step are heard e'en now within the camp.

The clang of bells, the bugle call—tramp of steeds and hurrying feet—
The ponderous artillery thundering down the crowded street—
The myriad flags—the shouts, the songs—Beauty's proud and bright array—
The "Stripes and Stars" from countless masts floating far adown the bay—

The greetings so fraternal borne sweetly on the air—
The gatherings round the altars, the solemn voice of prayer—

While high o'er all the anthem-peal of LIBERTY is heard—
Tell how deeply, tell how gloriously the nation's soul is stirred.

O God! the grandeur of this hour hath ne'er been seen on earth,
Since storm-rocked in old Faneuil Hall fair Freedom had her birth;
Since her beacons flamed at midnight, and at sound of signal horn
The yeomen went to Concord on *that other* April morn.

The cold dead Northern heart hath burst—and from its hot depths pour
The festering wrongs of weary years like waves on memory's shore;
The blows that fell on Sumner—by New-England unforgiven,
The outrage, and the murders, and the insults piled to heaven!

The tramp of marching legions—the crash of thousand drums,
And cannon's thunder mark the hour when *Retribution* comes;

And the Northern States like giants southward
move in awful form,
With the forces of all NATURE and GOD behind
the storm.

The loathsome monster ye have dragged up from
his slimy lair,
To be your *fitting emblem*—insulting God's free
air—
Shall fall! and 'neath the Northern heel be crush-
ed its crested head,
Ere yet along the slave-land is hushed the Yan-
kee's tread.

Too long *our* flag hath waved above the slaver's
cursèd marts,
Too long the man-thief mocked with it the hopes
of human hearts;
Take it now from 'neath his trampling — over
Southern field and flood
Bear it on! till ye have washed it all spotless in
his blood.

Ere again that flag home cometh, or is hushed the
Northern drum,
Every shackle shall be broken, and the SLAVE'S
REDEMPTION COME!

Dissembling *Compromise* no more shall rear her
serpent form;
For the forces of all NATURE and GOD are with
the storm.

Ocean deep be buried party feuds—broken every
party band;
Let each heart keep wide-open door—each strong
hand grasp a hand:
Let by-gones all be by-gones—pass around the
olive branch,
Then down upon the traitors like the Alpine ava-
lanche.

The Scotsman from his heatherhills—the "Emer-
ald Island's" sons—
The German from the Rhine-banks—Garibaldi's
chosen ones—
All who would crush oppression in the field or on
the throne,
March with us—and the Old World's heart beats
kindly 'gainst our own.

Heaven and earth are gazing on us! God begirt
us with his power;
We crowd the hopes of centuries into this passing
hour:

Skyward fling the starry banner, which shall nevermore be furled—
WE'RE MARCHING FOR HUMANITY! WE STRIKE FOR ALL THE WORLD!

TO OUR AMERICAN COUSINS.

ALL hail! Yankee Doodle, thou chief among nations!
What kingdom can swagger or talk tall like you;
What people so skilled are, in bombast and dodging,
Or to their engagements less faithful or true?

All hail thou proud banner—great herald of freedom!
Star-spangled indeed, but with stripes not a few;
What mockery that cry is — here mankind are equal!
While the slaves' groan reply that they freedom ne'er knew.

Great indeed is thy boasting, and fertile thy genius,
Still restless, and seeking for something's that's new;

Great, because yet untried, thou art vain and conceited,
A warrior, a statesman, a brave man are you.

Most men do grow wiser even as they grow older,
Some few become dotards as older they grow;
But a mighty Republic, scarce ripened to manhood,
Decaying in boyhood, is indeed a rare show.

Blush not, proud Columbia; let rivals still envy—
Your greatness and glory and fame *are your own*,
Your inventions and notions—hams and wood nutmegs,
Save by you discovered would never be known.

In war too triumphant—all nations excelling;
Thy innocent conquests cause nobody wrong;
No mourners for sweethearts, or fathers, or husbands,
Fort Sumter shall henceforth shine brightly in song!

Loud roared the dread cannon; *some say they were loaded—*
'Tis certain the powder made volumes of smoke—
Old gunners maintain *that the balls are still flying*,
But the young bloods declare that the thing was a joke.

They ask is it reason? For since the first battle
Men never have fought in this manner before;
Neither scratches nor bruises, nor have any been frightened,
Although thousands to witness stood thick on the shore.

While barbarous nations do fight and kill thousands,
What a glorious example is set by thy sons!
No danger can daunt them—they storm that fortress,
And when it is captured they spike all the guns.

Hard fighting there was, sure no mortal can doubt it,
The marksmen were keen and could hit to a hair;
But that ball never flew, could come up with the Yankee,
They dodged every bullet while high in the air.

Now warfare is shorn of all its dread terrors,
American science the secret has found,
By which mighty armies may fight on for ages,
And come off victorious without scratch or wound.

This plan has been tested and proved beyond question,
Fort Sumter was captured on this excellent plan;
All the troops there contending were covered with glory,
But neither victor nor vanquished have yet lost a man.

A patent, of course, will be speedily granted,
And Yankees henceforward will fight by this rule;
While the dotard old nations all over the world,
Will slaughter each other like so many fools.

Then hurrah for Columbia, most enlightened of nations,
Long, long may she fight and from bloodshed be free;
But, dear Sam, have a care, and provoke not the battle
With nations that jeer at your wise patentee.

Domestic arrangements, who dares to dispute them?
To adopt them, believe it, John Bull will be slow

And that ugly bayonet, when the charge is once
sounded,
Has seldom been dodged by the tact of the foe.
—Montreal Paper.

A PARODY—AFTER LEIGH HUNT.

BY UPSON DOWNS.

Jefferson Davis (may his tribe decrease!)
Awoke one night with ague in his knees;
Seeing within the moonlight of his room
A female form, resplendent as the moon;
Columbia, writing in a book of gold.
Exceeding brass had made the Davis bold,
And to the presence in the room he said:
"What writest thou?" The vision raised its head,
And with a look all dignity and calm,
Answered: "The names of those who love our
Uncle Sam."
"And is mine one?" said Davis. "Nay, not so,"
Replied Columbia. Davis spake more low,
But clearly still, and said: "I pray thee, then,
Write me the names of those who hate their fel-
low-men."

Columbia wrote and vanished. The next night
She came again, with her new list all right,
And showed the names humanity detest,
And lo! Jeff Davis' name led all the rest.

BEAUREGARD.

A HISTORICAL POEM.

The following ballad exhibits the constancy, truth, and devotion of a young knight of the olden time. We have another knight, a gallant soldier, who has proven his fidelity to the South, which he loves with all his heart. His batteries spoke for him in tones of thunder, at the bombardment of Sumter.—*Southern Paper.*

IN Pavia's bloody battle-field,
(As troubadours do sing,)
No nobler captive e'er did yield
Than Gaul's beloved king.

A prisoner in Italia's land,
One friend he mourns, I ween,
For fav'rite of his warrior band
Brave *Beauregard* had been.

Yet pined he not in gloomy cell,
Nor lay he with the slain;

A lady fair with magic spell
Had bound him in love's chain.

Aurelia! beautiful as day,
Was good as she was fair;
Her smile was ever bright as May,
Her presence banished care.

" Aurelia, sweetest! be but mine,
And such my love shall be,
That heaven's sunbeam ne'er may shine
On two so blest as we."

" Chevalier, list!" Aurelia cried,
" My heart now echoes each
Sweet word of pleading—yet thy bride
Through ordeal must thou reach.

" All nations say that sons of France
Are generous, brave, and gay;
They sigh and love, yet quickly dance
Each sober thought away.

" The man I fain would trust and love
No levity must show;
His soul must mirror truth above,
His heart no change must know."

By grief and dark despair opprest,
The warrior cries in anguish:
"O lady bright! my love attest,
And do not let me languish."

"Now, Beauregard!" Aurelia sighed,
"If, for six months to come,
To win me for thy faithful bride
Thou wilt remain but dumb!

"Mute to thy friends in sunny France,
Speechless 'neath thy roof,
Silent before each beauty's glance—
I ask no other proof.

"My willing hand I'll give to you—
Each throb of this fond heart—
And if your promise you keep true,
We never more shall part."

"Aurelia! I shall faithful be,"
The chevalier replied;
"These lips are sealed to all but thee,
My guerdon sweet—my bride!"

Back to his father's halls he sped:
"Welcome, my valiant son!

We thought thee numbered with the dead—
Quick to my arms now run!

"Ah! there's thy mother. See her tears
Of gratitude to One
Who saved thee through the mist of years—
Her only, much-loved son."

With moistened eye and frantic joy
Ah! hear that mother shriek:
"My long-lost son! my darling boy!
Speak to thy mother! speak!"

But faithful Beauregard is mute,
His friends bewail his doom;
Nor festive dance nor minstrel's lute
Can dissipate their gloom.

Physicians, famous in their art,
Prescribe, but all in vain,
The love which fired his faithful heart
Held o'er his tongue the rein.

The captive King at length set free
By sons of France with glory,
All welcome him—but grieved was he
To hear this hapless story.

King Francis, brave as any man,
  Was one whom spells might lure,
He daily sought each charlatan,
  Who Beauregard could cure.

Six months at length have passed away,
  And round the tidings ring;
"Aurelia is a bride this day,
  She's won by Pavia's King!"

Oh! saddened is poor Beauregard,
  And pallid is his cheek,
But yet resolved to keep his word,
  And die ere he should speak.

Just then a fortune-telling dame,
  Of skill and high renown,
Unto the court of Francis came,
  From distant foreign town.

She told the King to his young knight,
  She'd bring the gift of speech,
And by her potent arts that night
  His malady would reach.

"Speed, ye courtiers! seek my friend,"
  The King exclaims with glee,

"Here's one who promises to end
His silent misery."

With step reluctant, faint and slow,
Young Beauregard complies,
"Aurelia's lost!" 'mid tears of woe
His soul escapes in sighs!

What boots the friendly welcome shout,
Which King and courtiers raise?
Though peace and joy resound without,
A storm within now plays.

With downcast eye and blushing cheek,
The sybil took his hands:
Speak, Beauregard! my love, oh! speak!
Aurelia now commands."

"Aurelia!" "Yes, thy faithful one,
Who'll never from thee sever,
For nobly hast thou wooed and won
This heart, now thine for ever!"

King Francis crowned their wedding-day
With dowry rich and rare,
And heaven smiled with brightest ray
On this fond, faithful pair.

KATE LUBY F——.

A VOICE FROM SPAIN.

ODE TO ABRAHAM LINCOLN.

Translated from the Spanish of Carolina Coronado de Perry, by Martha Perry Lowe.

LINCOLN, I salute thee! conqueror thou art,
Chosen of the people's heart.
Traversing the mighty billows o'er
Of the wondrous, awful sea,
From America the free,
Thou hast reached unto this far-off Spanish shore.

Glorious exemplar of the Christian calling,
I have heard thy accents falling,
Heard thee raise thy voice against the tyrants' cause.
So the genius of the great,
Sovereign people of the State,
May preserve the volume of its sacred laws.

Wondrous book—the admiration of the ages!
In those solitudes, the pages
From the lofty soul of Washington were born—

Pages whose sublime commands,
Seizing with their reckless hands,
Bastard sons of liberty have rudely torn.

I behold thee calm, amid the tumult gazing,
Quailing not before the blazing
Of the traitors' fire within thy land begun.
They would in dishonor drag
At their feet the blushing flag,
Fluttering there before the fillibuster's gun.

My own ancestors, like thine of early story,
Saw of old thy country's glory.
Valiant men they were who sailed away from here,
Leaving traces all around,
Like thy names in history found;
Handing memories down to every coming year.

And I feel my longing spirit in me burning
With an infinite and tender yearning,
When I look upon the conquests of the brave—
Deeming they have served the end,
Only further to extend
The abhorred territory of the slave.

Ah! what will become of that great nation
yonder,
If the maddening clouds that wander,
Threatening all the heaven, should gather in their
sight?
Darkening in the azure sky,
With their shadows rising high—
What if they extinguish all the vivid light?

With a fixed and earnest eye that noble coun-
try seeing,
Whence my children drew their being
I do tremble for those stars upon the blue;
For my very life is blent
With the brightness they have lent,
And if they are waning, I am waning too.

But I listen to the Northern armies cheering,
Their huzzas and plaudits hearing,
Which they raise on high to herald thy increase;
And their ardor I do share,
Lifting up my humble prayer
For their liberty, their glory, and their peace.

And to thee, Señor, the hope of all the nation,
My good cheer and salutation
I would send amid the mighty billows' roar—

Send across the solemn sea,
To America the free,
Wafted by the breezes of the Spanish shore.

SONG OF THE SOUTHERN WOMEN.

O ABRAHAM LINCOLN! we call thee to hark
To the song we are singing, we Joans of Arc;
While our brothers are bleeding we fear not to bleed,
We'll face the Red Horror should there be need.
By our brothers we'll stand on the terrible field,
By our brothers we'll stand, and we'll ask for no shield;
By our brothers we'll stand as a torch in the dark,
To shine on thy treachery, we Joans of Arc.

Behold our free plumes of the wild eagle dark,
Behold them, and take our white brows for thy mark;
We fear not thy cannon, we heed not thy drum,
The deeper thy thunder the stronger we come.

Is woman a coward? No, no, she is brave!
Oh! nothing but love ever made her a slave;
In home's happy circle she's poetry's lark,
But threaten that home and she's Joan of Arc.

O Abraham Lincoln! we call thee to hark,
Thou Comet of Satan! thou Boast of the Dark!
Take off thy red shadow from Washington's land—
Back! back! for thy footstep is slavery's brand.
Future-eyed prophecy cries to thee, DOWN!
For she sees on thy forehead the hope of a Crown;
The fire that *sleeps* in our Southern eyes dark,
Would *lighten* in battle—we're Joans of Arc.

JULIA MILDRED.

APOCALYPSE.

"All Hail to the Stars and Stripes!"

LUTHER C. LADD.*

STRAIGHT to his heart the bullet crushed,
Down from his breast the red blood gushed,
And o'er his face a glory rushed.

* Killed at Baltimore, Md., April 19, 1861.

A sudden spasm rent his frame,
And in his ears there went and came
A sound as of devouring flame.

Which in a moment ceased, and then
The great light clasped his brows again,
So that they shone like Stephen's, when

Saul stood apart a little space,
And shook with shuddering awe to trace
God's splendor settling o'er his face.

Thus, like a king, erect in pride,
Raising his hands to heaven, he cried,
"All hail the Stars and Stripes!" and died.

Died grandly; but, before he fell,
(O blessedness ineffable!)
Vision apocalyptical

Was granted to him, and his eyes,
All radiant with glad surprise,
Looked forward through the centuries,

And saw the seeds that sages cast
In the world's soil in cycles past,
Spring up and blossom at the last:

Saw how the souls of men had grown,
And where the scythes of Truth had mown,
Clear space for Liberty's white throne;

Saw how, by sorrow tried and proved,
The last dark stains had been removed
For ever from the land he loved.

Saw Treason crushed, and Freedom crowned,
And clamorous faction gagged and bound,
Gasping its life out on the ground;

While over all his country's slopes
Walked swarming troops of cheerful hopes,
Which evermore to broader scopes

Increased, with power that comprehends
The world's weal in its own, and bends
Self-needs to large, unselfish ends.

Saw how, throughout the vast extents
Of earth's most populous continents,
She dropped such rare heart-affluence,

That, from beyond the farthest seas,
The wondering peoples thronged to seize
Her proffered pure benignities;

And how, of all her trebled host
Of widening empires, none could boast
Whose strength or love was uppermost,

Because they grew so equal there
Beneath the flag, which, *debonnaire*,
Waved joyous in the golden air;

Wherefore the martyr, gazing clear
Beyond the gloomy atmosphere
Which shuts us in with doubt and fear;

He, marking how her high increase
Ran greatening in perpetual lease
Through balmy years of odorous peace,

Greeted, in one transcendent cry
Of intense, passionate ecstacy,
The sight that thrilled him utterly;

Saluting, with most proud disdain
Of murder and of mortal pain,
The vision which shall be again.

So, lifted with prophetic pride,
Raised conquering hands to heaven, and cried,
"All hail the Stars and Stripes!" and died.

CLARENCE BUTLER.

UNDER THE WASHINGTON ELM,

CAMBRIDGE, APRIL 27, 1861.

BY OLIVER WENDELL HOLMES.

I.

EIGHTY years have passed, and more,
Since under the brave old tree,
Our fathers gathered in arms and swore
They would follow the sign their banners bore,
And fight till the land was free.

II.

Half of their work was done,
Half is left to do—
Cambridge, and Concord, and Lexington,
When the battle is fought and won,
What shall be told of you?

III.

Hark! 'tis the South wind moans—
Who are the martyrs down?
Ah! the marrow was true in your children's bones,
That sprinkled with blood the cursed stones
Of the murder-haunted town!

IV.

What if the storm-clouds blow ?
What if the green leaves fall ?
Better the crashing tempest's throe,
Than the army of worms that gnawed below ;
Trample them one and all !

V.

Then, when the battle is won,
And the land from traitors free,
Our children shall tell of the strife begun
When Liberty's second April sun
Was bright on our brave old tree !

COLONEL ELLSWORTH.

BY R. H. STODDARD.

IT fell upon us like a crushing woe,
Sudden and terrible. " Can it be ? " we said,
" That he from whom we hoped so much, is dead,
Most foully murdered ere he met the foe ? "

Why not? The men that would disrupt the State
By such base plots as theirs—frauds, thefts, and lies—
What code of honor do they recognize?
They thirst for blood to satisfy their hate,
Our blood: so be it; but for every blow
Woe shall befall them; not in their wild way,
But stern and pitiless, we will repay,
Until, like swollen streams, *their* blood shall flow:
And should we pause, the thought of ELLSWORTH slain,
Will steel our aching hearts to strike again!

May 24, 1861.

SCOTT AND THE VETERAN.

BY BAYARD TAYLOR.

I.

AN old and crippled veteran to the War Department came,
He sought the Chief who led him, on many a field of fame—

The Chief who shouted "Forward!" where'er his banner rose,
And bore its stars in triumph behind the flying foes.

II.

"Have you forgotten, General," the battered soldier cried,
"The days of eighteen hundred twelve, when I was at your side?
Have you forgotten Johnson, that fought at Lundy's Lane?
'Tis true I'm old and pensioned, but I want to fight again."

III.

"Have I forgotten?" said the Chief; "my brave old soldier, No!
And here's the hand I gave you then, and let it tell you so:
But you have done your share, my friend; you're crippled, old, and gray,
And we have need of younger arms and fresher blood to-day."

IV.

"But, General!" cried the veteran, a flush upon his brow;
"The very men who fought with us, they say are traitors now:
They've torn the flag of Lundy's Lane, our old red, white, and blue,
And while a drop of blood is left, I'll show that drop is true.

V.

"I'm not so weak but I can strike, and I've a good old gun
To get the range of traitors' hearts, and prick them one by one;
Your Minié rifles and such arms it a'nt worth while to try;
I couldn't get the hang of them, but I'll keep my powder dry!"

VI.

"God bless you, comrade!" said the Chief—"God bless your loyal heart!
But younger men are in the field, and claim to have their part.

They'll plant our sacred banner in each rebellious town,
And woe, henceforth, to any hand that dares to pull it down!"

VII.

"But, General!"—still persisting, the weeping veteran cried;
"I'm young enough to follow, so long as *you're* my guide:
And some, you know, must bite the dust, and that, at least, can I;
So, give the young ones place to fight, but me a place to die!

VIII.

"If they should fire on Pickens, let the colonel in command
Put me upon the rampart, with the flag-staff in my hand:
No odds how hot the cannon-smoke, or how the shells may fly,
I'll hold the Stars and Stripes aloft, and hold them till I die!

IX.

"I'm ready, General, so you let a post to me be given,
Where Washington can see me, as he looks from highest heaven,
And say to Putnam at his side, or, may be, General Wayne,
'There stands old Billy Johnson, that fought at Lundy's Lane!'"

X.

"And when the fight is hottest, before the traitors fly,
When shell and ball are screeching, and bursting in the sky,
If any shot should hit me, and lay me on my face,
My soul would go to Washington, and not to Arnold's place!"

May 18, 1861.

ELLSWORTH.

MAY 24, 1861.

BY WILLIAM H. BURLEIGH.

WHO keeps his faith in God and man,
By sore temptation unsubdued;
Who trusts the right and loves the good,
Lives long, however brief his span.

True life is measured not by days,
Nor yet by deeds, though bravely wrought—
Its truest gauge is noblest thought,
And this commands our highest praise.

So, though men say, "Alas! how brief
His course whose death we mourn to-day!"
The prescient soul must answer, "Nay—
Ye wrong him with this bitter grief."

What seems our loss hath this redress—
His life, by generous will and act,
No dream, but an eternal fact,
Is rounded into perfectness.

He *is*, not *was*: the pulse that beat
    But yesterday within his frame
    To-day is like a living flame
In every manly breast we meet.

Poured through a thousand hearts, the life
    That ebbed in his asserts its sway,
    An impulse that forbids delay
When Duty summons to the strife.

And hosts, by that grand impulse moved,
    With eager haste their weapons clasp,
    And swear to save from Treason's grasp
The country and the cause he loved.

So sanctified by martyr-blood,
    To us that cause is doubly dear;
    And who, remembering him, will fear
To stand for right, as ELLSWORTH stood?

For faith like his its like begets,
    And courage, though the hero die,
    Doth multiply and multiply,
In large excess of our regrets.

And thus one soul, that never swerved
From duty, fills a land with light;
And countless arms are nerved for fight
By one strong arm that death unnerved.

So, best . . . since so, the largest good
Results—nor need we sum the cost,
For lives so lost are never lost
To freedom saved by martyr-blood.

For him henceforth his country claims
The ground as holy where he sleeps,
And, like a loving mother, keeps
His name among her dearest names.

And when Love bids his monument
Lift its pure column to the air,
No fitter legend can it bear
Than his brave words: "I AM CONTENT!"

"Content, whatever fate be mine—
A sacred duty bids me go,
And though the issue none can know,
I hear and heed the voice divine.

"Content—since confident that He
To whom the sparrow's fall is known,
Will have some purpose of his own
Even in the fate of one like me." *

O golden words! O faith sublime!
O spirit breathing holy breath!
For such an one *there is no death*,
But crescent potencies through time!

And still where loyal arms roll back
The crimson tide of traitorous war,
His memory, like a beacon-star,
Shall shine above the battle's rack—

A flame, the patriot's heart to cheer,
And give new temper to his sword—
A fire, to blast the rebel horde
And melt their courage into fear.

* In the last letter addressed to his parents, penned but a few hours previous to his assassination, Col. Ellsworth says: "Whatever may happen, cherish the consolation that I was engaged in the performance of a sacred duty; and to-night, thinking over the probabilities of the morrow and the occurrences of the past, I am perfectly content to accept whatever my fortune may be, confident that he who noteth even the fall of a sparrow will have some purpose even in the fate of one like me."

And when—Rebellion's power subdued—
Shall dawn for us a better day,
When peace again resumes her sway
And links the bands of brotherhood—

From North to South, from East to West,
His name shall be a household word,
Revered and loved wherever heard,
And treasured with our worthiest.

So, for his land, the good he meant,
Won in the triumph of the right,
His spirit, starred with heaven's own light,
Once more shall say: "I AM CONTENT!"

PROMOTED.*

HUSHED be each sorrowing murmur,
And let no hot tear be shed,
As in slow march, with drooping standards,
Ye bear back the gallant dead.

* Colonel E. E. Ellsworth fell May twenty-fourth, 1861.

Dead! dead! with a death so royal
  That our full hearts dare not weep—
Gently lay the true and knightly
  To his holy, happy sleep.

It is well our sad blood-offering
  Should be so pure a breast,
That the coward's treacherous bullet
  Should find this stainless crest.

For among hero saints and martyrs
  Now to claim him bending down,
There is none bears a soul more loyal,
  None who wears a brighter crown.

Blessed they among the children
  Whom dear mother-land has nurst,
Whose joyous blood beneath her banner
  Gushes fullest, freest, first.

Wrap the flag he loved about him,
  Beside him place his maiden blade,
Fold the cold hands prayerfully
  Above the heart in stillness laid.

Happy hero! on the field promoted
  From colonel's tent to patriot's grave;

Bear to his rest the youthful martyr,
  Loved of the land he died to save.

New-York, May 24, 1861. RUFUS K. PHELPS.

THE DEATH OF ELLSWORTH.

A STAR has gone from the firmament,
  A sword from the altar ruddy;
There is silence of death in his fleecy tent
  And the banner is draped and bloody.

He fell alone, when the town was won;
  And the squadrons that breathless found him,
While over the hills broke the early sun,
  Saw the flag of the rebels around him.

In the flush of pride, when the blood was high,
  And the glory of youth upon him,
Still lingered a light in his glassy eye,
  And a smile when the death had won him.

How dabbled the skeins of his raven hair!
  The broad, high brow, how pallid!

How hushed the bugle of voice ; how fair
  The lips and the cheeks so calid !

And far away where the downs are white,
  And the dew on the prairie gleaming,
While the shimmer of dawn breaks over the night,
  A plighted woman is dreaming.

She thinks of a day when the war is still,
  And peace, like a river flowing,
And the harvest golden upon the hill,
  And the reapers away a-mowing :

How a glossy plume up the lane shall come,
  And a spur on the porch shall rattle,
And a voice that deafened the bugle and drum
  And ran down the ranks of battle,

Shall tell of perils that lead to fame,
  And of souls crushed out in the grapple,
And of soldiers returning, in peace, to claim
  Their loves in the village chapel.

Alas ! for the love that cannot die ;
  Alas ! for the forms that vanish ;
Alas ! for the hopes that are flushing high,
  And the dreams that the morning banish !

Where the Father of Nations sleeps entombed,
  In the willows gray and grouping,
The eagle of battles is raven plumed,
  And the flag of the Union drooping.

But the West is pouring her hardy Huns
  Where the bayonets flash and glitter,
And the boom of the funeral minute guns
  Stir the North clans hot and bitter.

The crape and the dusky plumes are doffed,
  The spear and the sabre gleaming,
The trampled banner is raised aloft,
  And the eagle is hoarsely screaming.

Her flight is strong as the dash of surge,
  And dark as the night her pinion;
The bat and the raven shall make their dirge
  In the homes of the Old Dominion.

The young are the brave and dutiful,
  The slain are the great in story;
But ghastly the lips of the beautiful,
  And the worm is the bride of glory.

George Alfred Townsend.

'EIN' FESTE BURG IST UNSER GOTT."

(*Luther's Hymn.*)

BY JOHN G. WHITTIER.

WE wait beneath the furnace blast
The pangs of transformation;
Not painlessly doth God recast
And mould anew the nation.
Hot burns the fire
Where wrongs expire;
Nor spares the hand
That from the land
Uproots the ancient evil.

The hand-breadth cloud the sages feared,
Its bloody rain is dropping;
The poison plant the fathers spared
All else is overtopping.
East, West, South, North,
It curses the earth:
All justice dies,
And fraud and lies
Live only in its shadow.

What gives the wheat-field blades of steel?
  What points the rebel cannon?
What sets the roaring rabble's heel
  On the old star-spangled pennon?
    What breaks the oath
    Of the men o' the South?
    What whets the knife
    For the Union's life?—
  Hark to the answer: SLAVERY!

Then waste no blows on lesser foes,
  In strife unworthy freemen;
God lifts to-day the veil, and shows
  The features of the demon!
    O North and South!
    Its victims both,
    Can ye not cry,
    "Let Slavery die!"
  And Union find in freedom?

What though the cast-out spirit tear
  The nation in his going?
We who have shared the guilt must share
  The pang of his o'erthrowing!
    Whate'er the loss,
    Whate'er the cross,

Shall they complain
Of present pain,
Who trust in God's hereafter?

For who that leans on His right arm
Was ever yet forsaken?
What righteous cause can suffer harm,
If He its part has taken?
Though wild and loud,
And dark the cloud,
Behind its folds
His hand upholds
The calm sky of to-morrow!

Above the maddening cry for blood,
Above the wild war-drumming,
Let Freedom's voice be heard, with good
The evil overcoming.
Give prayer and purse
To stay The Curse,
Whose wrong we share,
Whose shame we bear,
Whose end shall gladden Heaven!

In vain the bells of war shall ring
Of triumphs and revenges,

While still is spared the evil thing
  That severs and estranges.
    But, blest the ear
    That yet shall hear
    The jubilant bell
    That rings the knell
  Of Slavery for ever!

Then let the selfish lip be dumb,
  And hushed the breath of sighing;
Before the joy of peace must come
  The pains of purifying.
    God give us grace,
    Each in his place
    To bear his lot,
    And, murmuring not,
  Endure, and wait, and labor!

"GOD BLESS ABRAHAM LINCOLN."

BY CAROLINE A. MASON.

"GOD bless him!" Rally, voice and pen!
  Pass round the gracious word, and then
Let all the people say, "Amen!"

God bless him—'tis a simple word,
Yet who a sweeter ever heard,
Or one that more the pulses stirred?

God bless him—*God!* too weak and poor
Our human service; we implore
God's blessing—neither less nor more.

God *bless* him—with a large increase,
With righteousness that shall not cease,
With wisdom and His "perfect peace."

God bless *him*—over all the rest;
And of His mercy's sweet behest,
Give him the portion largest, best.

God bless him!—can we more?—in this,
The perfectness of human bliss,
All joy, all peace, all fulness is!

And so, God bless him! Once again
Take up the burden, voice and pen,
While all the people say, "Amen!"

Fitchburgh, Mass.

TO GENERAL BUTLER.

BY BAY STATE.

BEN Butler, my boy,
It gives me much joy,
Of your brave words and acts to hear.
So prompt and so quick,
You are truly a "brick,"
Knowing not the meaning of fear.

As a lawyer bold
We know you of old,
In many a "hard knotty case."
But now on the field,
Convinced you'll not yield:
You are just the man for the place.

Be true to your trust,
And bring to the dust
The rebels where'er they are found.
Inform them, dear Ben,
They've mistaken the men
If they think the North is not sound.

We know you are right,
Wherever you fight,
In upholding the Stripes and Stars.

We know they are wrong,
Where'er they belong,
Who follow the stripes and bars.

See to it our flag
Displaces that rag,
Symbolic of despot and slave;
From Georgia to Maine
It must wave again
" O'er the land of the free and the brave."

We will anxiously wait
To hear of your fate,
Entreating God's blessing on you;
For one thing we know,
" Come weal or come woe,"
To the Union you'll ever be true.

A FRAGMENT—CABINET COUNCIL.

LINCOLN—[*solus; asleep in a rocking-chair—after a pause, springs up suddenly.*]
Give me another Scotch cap; wrap me in a military cloak!

Have mercy, Jeff. Davis! Soft—I did but dream!
[*Loud knocking heard at the door.*]
Who knocks thus loudly?

SEWARD—[*without.*] 'Tis I, my Lord! the White House cock;
Thrice have I crowed since the day hath broke.

[*Enter Seward, Chase, Bates, Blair, Cameron, and Welles.*]

CAMERON—How doth my good Lord?

LINCOLN—Indifferently well, methinks, good Coz.
That confection of hominy and hog, which, as my wont,
Late on yester eve I ate, did most wofully affect me.
Have I no leech among my councillors chosen,
Who can minister to a body diseased? Alas! my friends!
Bred to the chicane of the law, what know ye of the leap
And bounds of rebellious blood by fitful fever stirred?

BATES—My Liege, as I glanced o'er the morning prints,
In which our glories are duly and at length set forth,
Methought much praise was given to a medicament
Yclept in foreign lore—Cephalic Pills!

LINCOLN—Away with this nostrum—I'll none of it!
For know ye, I bought a box from a harum-scarum boy,
Whom I encountered on our Western train, and who
Cried—God wot!—"Old Abe, buy some Pills?"
These I bought, and tried, and got no better fast.
BLAIR—You'd scarce expect one of my age
To speak in public on the stage. Yet I can but think
'Tis not the *con*fection, but the *de*fection of the Southern tier,
Which pains our Liege's——
LINCOLN—Ass! knave! think you so?
Know you not, my babbling Coz, that this *de*fection
Is all gammon?—the crisis is but artificial!
CHASE—We know it well; would we could forget it;
Yet, your Excellency, I read in some fool
Southern paper—called, I know not what—
The *Mail*, the *Mercury*, or some such absurdity—
That there is much feeling down in their unsightly swamps,
Where Afric's wrongs smell rank to heaven.
LINCOLN—What then! Let them howl!—You know full well,
That, cry as they may, there's nobody hurt!

Oh! how I do despise a peevish, complaining people—
A people who know not which side their bread is buttered.
Misguided people! who would fain tear away three stripes—
Two of red and one of white—from our Star-Spangled Banner.

SEWARD—[*aside.*] Long may it wave!

WELLES—O'er the land of the free!

BATES—And the home of the brave!

LINCOLN—And imagine they founded a new nation!
And now yon fighting Colonel Davis,
With his ragged ragamuffin crew, loudly swears
He'll sit in this very chair wherein we sit—
Save the mark!—in spite of Wool or Scott.
Friends, farewell! yet take something ere ye go
Leave me to myself, that I may court the drowsy god.
Watch well the door, that no foul traitors enter
With machines infernal, or throated revolving pistol.
Spread yourselves, and lose no opportunity to tell
Th' expectant people that all is going well;
And while, reluctant, ye admit the Southern feeling,

Urge and declare that 'tis marvellous consoling,
That nothing is hurting any body. There, go!
Stand not on the order of your going, but go at
once.

[*Seward and others bow and depart.*]

New Jerusalem! is this happiness? When erst
I dreamt of might, majesty, and power; when, in
days gone by,
An humble splitter of rails, wearing but one shirt
a week;
Or, when in reverie, I leaned in listless mood
O'er the oar (ha! a pun) of the slow-gliding broad-
horn,
And thought of the powerful and rich of earth,
And, envious, contrasted their gay feasts and revels
With our simple joys, our humble shuckings and
possum hunts,
Our apple-bees and quilting frolics—alack-a-day!
As Shakespeare says in his Paradise Lost, I sadly
feel
That "distance lends enchantment to the view."

—*Charleston Mercury.*

UPON THE HILL BEFORE CENTREVILLE.

JULY TWENTY-FIRST, 1861.

BY GEORGE H. BOKER.

I'LL tell you what I heard that day:
I heard the great guns, far away,
Boom after boom. Their sullen sound
Shook all the shuddering air around;
And shook, ah me! my shrinking ear,
And downward shook the hanging tear
That, in despite of manhood's pride,
Rolled o'er my face a scalding tide.
And then I prayed. O God! I prayed,
As never stricken saint, who laid
His hot cheek to the holy tomb
Of Jesus, in the midnight gloom.

"What saw I?" Little. Clouds of dust;
Great squares of men, with standards thrust
Against their course; dense columns crowned
With billowing steel. Then, bound on bound,
The long black lines of cannon poured
Behind the horses, streaked and gored
With sweaty speed. Anon shot by,
Like a lone meteor of the sky,

A single horseman; and he shone
His bright face on me, and was gone.
All these with rolling drums, with cheers,
With songs familiar to my ears,
Passed under the far-hanging cloud,
And vanished, and my heart was proud!

For mile on mile the line of war
Extended; and a steady roar,
As of some distant stormy sea,
On the south-wind came up to me.
And high in air, and over all,
Grew, like a fog, that murky pall,
Beneath whose gloom of dusty smoke
The cannon flamed, the bombshell broke,
And the sharp rattling volley rang,
And shrapnel roared, and bullets sang,
And fierce-eyed men, with panting breath,
Toiled onward at the work of death.
I could not see, but knew too well,
That underneath that cloud of hell,
Which still grew more by great degrees,
Man strove with man in deeds like these.

But when the sun had passed his stand
At noon, behold! on every hand

The dark brown vapor backward bore,
And fainter came the dreadful roar
From the huge sea of striving men.
Thus spoke my rising spirit then:
"Take comfort from that dying sound,
Faint heart, the foe is giving ground!"
And one, who taxed his horse's powers,
Flung at me, "Ho! the day is ours!"
And scoured along. So swift his pace,
I took no memory of his face.
Then turned I once again to Heaven;
All things appeared so just and even;
So clearly from the highest Cause
Traced I the downward-working laws—
Those moral springs, made evident,
In the grand, triumph-crowned event.
So half I shouted, and half sang,
Like Jephtha's daughter, to the clang
Of my spread, cymbal-striking palms,
Some fragments of thanksgiving psalms.

Meanwhile a solemn stillness fell
Upon the land. O'er hill and dell
Failed every sound. My heart stood still,
Waiting before some coming ill.
The silence was more sad and dread,
Under that canopy of lead,

Than the wild tumult of the war
That raged a little while before.
All nature, in her work of death,
Paused for one last, despairing breath;
And, cowering to the earth, I drew
From her strong breast my strength anew.

When I arose, I wondering saw
Another dusty vapor draw,
From the far right, its sluggish way
Toward the main cloud, that frowning lay
Against the western sloping sun;
And all the war was re-begun,
Ere this fresh marvel of my sense
Caught from my mind significance.
And then—why ask me? O my God!
Would I had lain beneath the sod,
A patient clod, for many a day,
And from my bones and mouldering clay
The rank field grass and flowers had sprung,
Ere the base sight, that struck and stung
My very soul, confronted me,
Shamed at my own humanity.
O happy dead! who early fell,
Ye have no wretched tale to tell
Of causeless fear and coward flight,
Of victory snatched beneath your sight,

Of martial strength and honor lost,
Of mere life bought at any cost,
Of the deep, lingering mark of shame,
For ever scorched on brow and name,
That no new deeds, however bright,
Shall banish from men's loathful sight!
Ye perished in your conscious pride,
Ere this vile scandal opened wide
A wound that cannot close nor heal.
Ye perished steel to levelled steel,
Stern votaries of the god of war,
Filled with his godhead to the core!
Ye died to live, these lived to die,
Beneath the scorn of every eye!
How eloquent your voices sound
From the low chambers under ground!
How clear each separate title burns
From your high set and laurelled urns!
While these, who walk about the earth,
Are blushing at their very birth!
And, though they talk, and go, and come,
Their moving lips are worse than dumb.
Ye sleep beneath the valley's dew,
And all the nation mourns for you;
So sleep till God shall wake the lands!
For angels, armed with fiery brands,
Await to take you by the hands.

The right-hand vapor broader grew ;
It rose, and joined itself unto
The main cloud with a sudden dash.
Loud and more near the cannon's crash
Came toward me, and I heard a sound
As if all hell had broken bound—
A cry of agony and fear.
Still the dark vapor rolled more near,
Till at my very feet it tossed,
The van-ward fragments of our host.
Can man, Thy image, sink so low,
Thou, who hast bent Thy tinted bow
Across the storm and raging main ;
Whose laws both loosen and restrain
The powers of earth, without whose will
No sparrow's little life is still ?
Was fear of hell, or want of faith,
Or the brute's common dread of death
The passion that began a chase,
Whose goal was ruin and disgrace ?
What tongue the fearful sight may tell ?
What horrid nightmare ever fell
Upon the restless sleep of crime—
What history of another time—
What dismal vision, darkly seen
By the stern-featured Florentine,

Can give a hint to dimly draw
The likeness of the scene I saw?
I saw, yet saw not. In that sea,
That chaos of humanity,
No more the eye could catch and keep
A single point, than on the deep
The eye may mark a single wave,
Where hurrying myriads leap and rave.
Men of all arms, and all costumes,
Bare-headed, decked with broken plumes;
Soldiers and officers, and those
Who wore but civil-suited clothes;
On foot or mounted—some bestrode
Steeds severed from their harnessed load;
Wild mobs of white-topped wagons, cars,
Of wounded, red with bleeding scars;
The whole grim panoply of war
Surged on me with a deafening roar!
All shades of fear, disfiguring man,
Glared through their faces' brazen tan.
Not one a moment paused, or stood
To see what enemy pursued.
With shrieks of fear, and yells of pain,
With every muscle on the strain,
Onward the struggling masses bore.
Oh! had the foemen lain before,
They'd trampled them to dust and gore,

And swept their lines and batteries
As autumn sweeps the windy trees!
Here one cast forth his wounded friend,
And with his sword or musket-end
Urged on the horses; there one trod
Upon the likeness of his God,
As if 'twere dust; a coward here
Grew valiant with his very fear,
And struck his weaker comrade prone,
And struggled to the front alone.
All had one purpose, one sole aim,
That mocked the decency of shame,
To fly, by any means to fly;
They cared not how, they asked not why.
I found a voice. My burning blood
Flamed up. Upon a mound I stood;
I could no more restrain my voice
Than could the prophet of God's choice.
"Back, animated dirt!" I cried,
"Back, on your wretched lives, and hide
Your shame beneath your native clay!
Or if the foe affrights you, slay
Your own base selves; and, dying, leave
Your children's tearful cheeks to grieve,
Not quail and blush, when you shall come,
Alive, to their degraded home!

Your wives will look askance with scorn
Your boys, and infants yet unborn,
Will curse you to God's holy face!
Heaven holds no pardon in its grace
For cowards. Oh! are such as ye
The guardians of our liberty?
Back, if one trace of manhood still
May nerve your arm and brace your will!
You stain your country in the eyes
Of Europe and her monarchies!
The despots laugh, the peoples groan;
Man's cause is lost and overthrown!
I curse you, by the sacred blood
That freely poured its purple flood
Down Bunker's heights, on Monmouth's plain,
From Georgia to the rocks of Maine!
I curse you, by the patriot band
Whose bones are crumbling in the land!
By those who saved what these had won—
In the high name of Washington!"
Then I remember little more.
As the tide's rising waves, that pour
Over some low and rounded rock,
The coming mass, with one great shock,
Flowed o'er the shelter of my mound,
And raised me helpless from the ground.

As the huge shouldering billows bear,
Half in the sea and half in air,
A swimmer on their foaming crest,
So the foul throng beneath me pressed,
Swept me along, with curse and blow,
And flung me—where, I ne'er shall know.

When I awoke, a steady rain
Made rivulets across the plain;
And it was dark—oh! very dark.
I was so stunned as scarce to mark
The ghostly figures of the trees,
Or hear the sobbing of the breeze
That flung the wet leaves to and fro.
Upon me lay a dismal woe,
A boundless, superhuman grief,
That drew no promise of relief
From any hope. Then I arose,
As one who struggles up from blows
By unseen hands; and as I stood
Alone, I thought that God was good,
To hide, in clouds and driving rain,
Our low world from the angel train,
Whose souls filled heroes when the earth
Was worthy of their noble birth.
By that dull instinct of the mind,
Which leads aright the helpless blind,

I struggled onward, till the dawn
Across the eastern clouds had drawn
A narrow line of watery gray;
And full before my vision lay
The great dome's gaunt and naked bones
Beneath whose crown the nation thrones
Her queenly person. On I stole,
With hanging head and abject soul,
Across the high embattled ridge,
And o'er the arches of the bridge.
So freshly pricked my sharp disgrace,
I feared to meet the human face,
Skulking, as any woman might,
Who'd lost her virtue in the night,
And sees the dreadful glare of day
Prepare to light her homeward way,
Alone, heart-broken, shamed, undone,
I staggered into Washington!

Since then long sluggish days have passed,
And on the wings of every blast
Have come the distant nations' sneers
To tingle in our blushing ears.
In woe and ashes, as was meet,
We wore the penitential sheet.
But now I breathe a purer air,
And from the depths of my despair

Awaken to a cheering morn,
Just breaking through the night forlorn,
A morn of hopeful victory.
Awake, my countrymen, with me!
Redeem the honor which you lost,
With any blood, at any cost!
I ask not how the war began,
Nor how the quarrel branched and ran
To this dread height. The wrong or right
Stands clear before God's faultless sight.
I only feel the shameful blow,
I only see the scornful foe,
And vengeance burns in every vein
To die, or wipe away the stain.
The war-wise hero of the West,
Wearing his glories as a crest,
Of trophies gathered in your sight,
Is arming for the coming fight.
Full well his wisdom apprehends
The duty and its mighty ends;
The great occasion of the hour,
That never lay in human power
Since over Yorktown's tented plain
The red cross fell, nor rose again.
My humble pledge of faith I lay,
Dear comrade of my school-boy day,

Before thee, in the nation's view,
And if thy prophet prove untrue,
And from our country's grasp be thrown
The sceptre and the starry crown,
And thou, and all thy marshalled host
Be baffled, and in ruin lost;
Oh! let me not outlive the blow
That seals my country's overthrow!
And, lest this woeful end come true,
Men of the North, I turn to you.
Display your vaunted flag once more,
Southward your eager columns pour!
Sound trump, and fife, and rallying drum;
From every hill and valley come.
Old men, yield up your treasured gold!
Can liberty be priced and sold?
Fair matrons, maids, and tender brides,
Gird weapons to your lovers' sides;
And, though your hearts break at the deed,
Give them your blessing and God speed;
Then point them to the field of flame,
With words like those of Sparta's dame;
And when the ranks are full and strong,
And the whole army moves along,
A vast result of care and skill,
Obedient to the master will;

And your young hero draws the sword,
And gives the last commanding word
That hurls your strength upon the foe—
Oh! let them need no second blow.
Strike, as your fathers struck of old,
Through summer's heat and winter's cold,
Through pain, disaster, and defeat;
Through marches tracked with bloody feet;
Through every ill that could befall
The holy cause that bound them all!
Strike as they struck for liberty!
Strike as they struck to make you free!
Strike for the crown of victory!

THE MODERN GILPIN.

A BALLAD OF BULL RUN.

WILL RUSSELL was a writer rare,
Of genius and renown,
A war-trained correspondent he
From famous London town.

On Indian and Crimean coasts
He wrote of guns and drums,

And now as through our land he posts,
  To Washington he comes.

Will Russell said to chosen friend:
"Though four months I have been
In search of some great Yankee fight,
  No skrimmage have I seen.

"To-morrow's sun will see a fight
  On Bull Run's banks, they say;
So there, my friend, we'll early go,
  All in a *two-'oss shay.*

"I'll also take a saddle-horse
  To bear the battle's brunt,
Whereon, in my Crimean style,
  I'll see the fight *in front.*

"And I will don the coolest of
  My Himalayan suits—
My belt, felt hat, revolver, and
  My old East-Indian boots.

"Fresh stores of pens I'll surely need,
  And foolscap, too, I think;

And in one holster snugly thrust
  A pint of Dovell's ink.

"While in the bottom of the gig
  We'll stow the choice Bordeaux,
And eke this bottle of *cold tea*,
  To cool us off, you know!

"And for that, in this heathen land,
  The grub is all a sham,
I've here wrapped up some sausage, too,
  And sandwiches of 'am.

"Experience on Crimean shores
  Has taught me how to forage,
And how these creature-comforts tend
  To keep up martial courage."

Smack went his lips at thought thereof—
  Off rolled the Yankee gig,
Before the shouts and rolling whites
  Of starers, small and big!

Like clouds of dust his spirits rise,
  While merry cracks the whip;
The led-horse pranced and "bobbed around"
  Like porpoise round a ship.

The Long Bridge planks jumped up and down
 In sympathetic jig;
They little thought he would return
 Minus the "creaking gig."

That rotten Rubicon is passed,
 And likewise frowning "Runyon,"
Its outlines marked with many a black
 Columbiad on its trunnion.

Past fields where just the day before
 The harvest-scythe was sweeping,
They rushed where soon its human sheaves
 Death's sickle would be reaping!

As rise the distant cannon's tones,
 So mounts his martial ardor,
His thoughts half on the work "in front,"
 Half on his meagre larder

At length he's there at Centreville!
 In sight and sound of what
He came so far to see and sketch,
 Where rained the shell and shot!

But ere he ventures, careful soul,
 To reach that scene of death,

He seeks a cool and shady place,
" To give his horses breath."

Then forth he draws the precious stores—
Cold tea, Bordeaux, and 'am—
Mid cannon-shots and bottle-pops,
Enjoys his lunch and dram.

The dubious issue of the fight
Contents him with his seat,
Until a courier from the field
Reports the foe's retreat!

Up sprang Will Russell from the charms
Of tea and 'am so vile—
His toilet for "the front" prepares,
In his Crimean style.

"My 'oss! my 'oss! quick, bring it me!
What would the *Thunderer* say,
If they should end this Bull Run fight,
While I lunch in my *shay?*"

His "Indian" sack hangs down and hides
Each short and sturdy limb;
His hat o'erhangs his jolly form
With amplitude of brim.

Beneath its shade, his round, red face
  Flames like St. George's banner;
While from its rim, in *havelock* style,
  A buff and red bandanna

In guise like this he grandly mounts,
  And starts in warlike trot,
That *did not* turn to gallop as
  He neared the deadly spot.

But, lo! a motley frightened crowd
  Before him doth appear,
Of such as ever follow camps,
  All hurrying to the rear.

And pushing through this heaving mass
  Of human breakers, soon
He found himself 'mid reeling ranks,
  Battalion and platoon!

But 'mid that frightened crowd, he says
  He only kept his wits,
And puffs, and scolds, and wonders, too,
  What trouble "gave them fits!"

I do declare! What means all this?
  What has your victory nipped?

Why run you so ?" the sole reply
Was panted forth, " We're whipped !"

" Dear me ! I fain would get in front !
How would the people stare,
If Fame should ask my whereabouts,
And echo say, " *The rear !*"

" You cravens, stand ! *why do* you run ?
Return to the assault !"
Bang ! bang ! a shell bursts o'er his head—
Will Russell calls a halt !

" Aw ! that *was* near ! no further need
For me to make researches—
I'll simply book what I have seen,
Behind yon grove of birches."

Bang ! bang ! " Aw ! there's another shell !
And one that is a screamer !
And, let me think—I must leave now,
To write by Wednesday's steamer !

" And though my steed has come to-day
Full thirty miles and better,
Needs must he now to take me back,
To mail my battle-letter ! "

He turns his horse; both are afloat
  On the retreating wave!
But as he struggles back, he scoffs
  In words—not accents brave.

To clear the road and let him pass,
  He hails each runaway,
But their respect for *rank*, alas!
  Is broke and done away!

Wagon and cart, and man and beast
  All in the turnpike jammed;
Mess pork and hams, and shot and grain,
  No thoroughfare so dammed!

The dainty stores that fed "the staff"
  Mixed with the private's fare!
Sad waste! "Oh! what, my countrymen,
  A falling off was there!"

The teamsters "cut and ran" and left,
  No *traces* you could find,
While those afoot from horsemen feared,
  A dreadful "cut behind!"

"The cavalry!" at that dread sound
  Will's courage was bereft him;

Although he tried by valiant words
  To show it had not left him.

And eke before his mental eye
  The dreadful vision rose,
Of that warm suit the Southern press
  Had threatened him for clothes!

"That threat! when 'tis so 'orrid 'ot—
  Beyond East-Indian weather!
How my too solid flesh would melt
  In suit of tar and feather!"

His anxious looks, yet valiant words,
  Make many jeer and hoot him,
While every random shot he fears
  Is some attempt to shoot him.

While thus he trembles for his life,
  By coward taunt and curse,
So, to his eye, each ambulance
  Seems an untimely hearse!

At each artillery "thud" he hears,
  Up close his legs he tucks,
Then down upon his saddle-bow
  His anxious visage ducks!

And eke behind his Indian sack
Swells in balloon-like manner,
While flaps and flies around his neck,
The buff and red bandanna!

Again he's back at Centreville,
In search of friend and gig;
" They are not here! nor 'am, nor tea—
They're just the things to prig.

" Oh! for a glass of wine, or slice
Of those fine wasted 'ams!—
But though there's plenty on the road,
They're no longer Uncle Sam's!

" So now for Washington, my steed
It is no use to whine;
You brought me here to see a fight,
Now take me back to dine!"

A sudden squad of fugitives
Here through the village fled;
And Bill's great fancy for the front
Soon placed him at their head.

But as he leads the flying herd
Adown a hill's decline,

Behold, across the road drawn up
  A regiment in line!

"What brings you here?" the Colonel shouts,
  "Back! back! I say. I'll shoot
The coward that across my ranks
  Would dare to place his foot!"

The herd recoils, save Russell wild,
  Who, fumbling in his vest:
"But, sir—you know!—I'm English! Come!
  You must not me arrest!

"I have a pass—aw! here it is!
  'Tis signed by General Scott—
Don't keep me here!" "Pass this man up!"
  Replied the Colonel, hot.

Nor time lost Will, as off he dashed,
  In sudden bolt that snapped
A loop of sack and havelock both,
  That now far rearward flapped!

At Fairfax Court-House next he stops,
  To breathe his horse and sup;
But here his rest by Boniface
  Is quickly broken up.

Quoth he: "They fear Virginia's horse?
Well may they, stranger, when
These mountain riders number now
Full twenty thousand men!"

"Good heavens! no?—but do they though?"
Our startled hero cries;
Then off again, though cruel need,
To Washington he flies!

Night finds him bravely spurring on,
Past wood, and grove, and thicket,
With brave words frequent cheering up
Each watchful, anxious picket.

"What news? What news?" they all do shout;
Says Russell in reply:
"It is no rout! the army's safe!
Keep up your heart—don't fly!"

"Stop! stop! Bill Russell! tell us why,"
Loud after him they bawl,
"If all is safe, you run so fast,
Or why you run at all?"

Yet on *he* flies; up hill, down dale,
In very ghostlike manner,

While ever rearward flaps and flies
The buff and red bandanna!

The night wanes on, the moon is up,
And soon our correspondent,
Though near his goal, with new-born fears
Grew suddenly despondent.

"The guards are set upon the bridge.
Dear me, what fate is mine!
They'll hail me soon, and I may die
And give no countersign!"

His fears are vain, that veteran name
Is good, as you'll agree,
(As has been often said before,)
To pass him through, *Scott* free.

At last he's safe upon the bridge!
He sees the lights of town
Mirrored in broad Potomac's tide,
Hangs brightly dripping down..

Then droops his head, then droops his steed,
In sympathetic manner;
Then droops his sack, then droops also
The buff and red bandanna.

Can this be he that o'er these planks
  At morning dashed so trig,
Revisiting beneath the moon
  In such a dismal rig?

The bridge is passed! and he again
  Resumes his martial port,
And swells, and puffs, and comforts all
  With words of valiant sort.

But sudden from the rising clouds
  A vivid lightning flash.
"The foe!" he cries, and fearful lists
  To hear the cannon's crash.

He's off again, up Fourteenth street!
  Once more, like ghostly banner,
Behind him dimly flaps and flies
  The buff and red bandanna.

His rooms are reached, he bolts his door,
  When lo! before his eyes
A midnight supper ready spread,
  To which he instant flies.

No time, by doffing hat or dress,
  To balk his famished jaws,

But, Cassius-like, he "plunges in,
  Accoutred as he was!"

Sausage, and cheese, and 'am again,
  With draughts of wine between;
Down that vast throat of British gauge,
  In quick procession seen!

What grunts of bliss beneath that hat,
  O'er this unlooked-for manna!
While, as he munched, still rose and fell
  The buff and red bandanna.

At last he's full; but quickly now
  His brain is all astir,
To forge fit bolts of caustic for
  His chief, the *Thunderer*.

His pen is drawn, and o'er his sheet
  Fast its vocation plies,
In telling what he *thought* he saw
  Wherein his genius *lies*.

But soon the inspiration's o'er;
  With wine and sausage pressed,
His eye-lids close, his burly head
  Down drops upon his breast.

Hark to the thunders of his snore,
In deep bassoon-like manner!
While with each swell still rose and fell
The buff and red bandanna.

Rest, Russell, rest! thy race is o'er;
And well you won it too;
For no such time was ever made
Since days of Waterloo.

Now let us sing in jolly ring
Great Russell's martial spree;
When next he goes to see a fight,
May he *get there* to see.

Ye poets, who may sing some day,
In strains rich, racy, full,
The race from Bull Run, don't forget
The run of Mr. Bull.

CHANTICLEER.

THE TEAMSTERS' PANIC.

BY WALTER ANONYM.

AT Bull Run, ere the sun was low,
'Twas man to man and blow for blow,
For fierce and furious was the foe,
And deadly was the rivalry.

But Bull Run saw another sight,
When all the teamsters, pale with fright,
And panic-stricken, took to flight,
Led by the British chivalry!

With sword and jack-knife fast arrayed,
Each teamster drew his valiant blade,
And furious every dray-horse neighed,
Dreading the Black Horse cavalry.

Now parts the trace, by jack-knife riven;
Now rush the steeds, by panic driven;
And all the road, by half-past seven,
Showed dustily and gravelly.

But thicker yet the dust shall fly,
As rank and file go scrambling by,

And louder yet shall Russell cry,
  "We're gone! we're gone! it's all o-ver!"

'Tis morn, but scarce yon southern sun
Hath tipped the spires of Washington,
When in they tumble, one by one,
  Russell ahead of Doll-i-ver.

The panic deepens. Save! who can.
When life's at stake a man's a man;
Most gallant he who leads the van.
  Lo! *Russell leads the whole of 'em!*

Ah! few, to-day, in camp shall meet;
The sidewalks shall be tent and sheet.
In every alley, lane, and street,
  They slumber, every soul of 'em.

THE RUN FROM MANASSAS JUNCTION.

YANKEE DOODLE went to war,
  On his little pony;
What did he go fighting for,
  Everlasting goney!

Yankee Doodle was a chap
  Who bragged and swore tarnation,
He stuck a feather in his cap,
  And called it Federation.
        Yankee Doodle, etc.

Yankee Doodle, he went forth
  To conquer the seceders,
All the journals of the North,
  In most ferocious leaders,
Breathing slaughter, fire, and smoke,
  Especially the latter,
His rage and fury to provoke,
  And vanity to flatter.
        Yankee Doodle, etc.

Yankee Doodle, having floored
  His separated brothers,
He reckoned his victorious sword
  Would turn against us others,
Secession first he would put down,
  Wholly and for ever;
And afterward, from Britain's crown,
  He Canada would sever.
        Yankee Doodle, etc.

England offering neutral sauce
  To goose as well as gander,
Was what made Yankee Doodle cross,
  And did inflame his dander.
As though with choler drunk he fumed,
  And threatened vengeance martial,
Because Old England had presumed
  To steer a course impartial.
        Yankee Doodle, etc.

Yankee Doodle bore in mind,
  When warfare England harassed,
How he, unfriendly and unkind,
  Beset her and embarrassed;
He put himself in England's place,
  And thought this injured nation
Must view his trouble with a base
  Vindictive exultation.
        Yankee Doodle, etc.

We for North and South alike
  Entertain affection;
These for negro slavery strike;
  Those for forced protection.
Yankee Doodle is the pot,
  Southerner the kettle;

Equal morally, if not
  Men of equal mettle.
      Yankee Doodle, etc.

Yankee Doodle, near Bull Run
  Met his adversary,
First he thought the fight he'd won,
  Fact proved quite contrary.
Panic-struck he fled, with speed
  Of lightning glib with unction,
Of slippery grease, in full stampede,
  From famed Manassas Junction.
      Yankee Doodle, etc.

As he bolted, no ways slow,
  Yankee Doodle hallooed,
"We are whipped!" and fled, although
  No pursuer followed.
Sword and gun right slick he threw
  Both away together,
In his cap, to public view,
  Showing the white feather.
      Yankee Doodle, etc.

Yankee Doodle, Doodle, do,
  Whither are you flying?

"A cocked hat we've been licked into,
  And knocked to Hades," crying?
Well, to Canada, sir-ree,
  Now that, by secession,
I am driven up a tree,
  To seize that there possession.
      Yankee Doodle, etc.

Yankee Doodle, be content,
  You've had a lenient whipping;
Court not further punishment
  By enterprise of stripping
Those neighbors, whom if you assail,
  They'll surely whip you hollow;
Moreover, when you've turned your tail,
  Won't hesitate to follow.
      Yankee Doodle, etc.

Ye LONDONNE TIMES CORRESPONDENTE—HIS BULLE RUNNE LETTERRE.

"BULLE RUNNE, July ye twenty-firste;
  Welle, here am I, alle righte,
And just returning from wytnessinge
  Ye famouse Bulle Runne fighte."

"There was no fighte, there was no Bulle,
Unlesse itte mighte bee mee;
And I the onlie manne to runne,
At leaste thatte I could see.

"I satte me on a dystante hylle,
Fulle fyfteene myles awaye,
Thatte I mighte see ye soldierees kille,
Iffe anie came mye waye.

"I hadde a branne newe telescope,
And a bottelle of olde Porte,
Wytthe sandewytches, inne case I founde
Ye provenderre ranne shorte.

"Ande soone I sawe a monstrouse crowde
Fulle fyfteene myles awaye,
And cannonnes there were roaringe loude,
And muskettes inne fulle playe.

"I satte mee there fromme earlie dawne
Untille ye settynge sunne,
And thenne I thoughte thatte certaynelie
Ye battelle muste bee done.

"I sawe no fighte, butte I muste write
As iffe I sawe itte alle,

Thoughe reallie I do believe,
Therre was no fighte atte alle.

"And thysse itte is mye judgemente,
Afteere carefulle studie mayde,
Thatte one syde is a cowarde,
And ye otherre is afrayde.

"I wysshe you woulde lette mee come home—
I'm tyred of all thysse bustle;
I wysshe no more ye worlde to roame,
Youres truly, BILLIE RUSSELLE."

THE CAPTURED EPAULETTE.

OH! we've beaten them gallantly! back from our soil;
We have hurled the invader, and taken his spoil;
And ghastly with death-wounds, all over the plain
Of Manassas, are lying the heaps of the slain;
We count them by thousands—for never before
Has our sod been so steeped and so reddened with gore.

We have taken us trophies—our swords and our
knives,
And our bullets have reaped us a harvest of lives;
The cannon they boasted, of deadliest powers,
Why, all of the best and the grandest are ours;
They will want to rejoice o'er the victory won!
And I wonder if Washington musters a gun.

We captured their knights by the hundred—they
ran,
As only an athlete or pickpocket can;
We pounced on their arms and their stores, and,
in fine,
We took from them every thing, even their wine;
The "champagne" and "heidsieck" to drink to
our fall—
And the bracelets they bought for us, handcuffs
and all!

But the trophy of trophies! oh! heard you it not?
Was the one that we gained from the shoulder of
Scott.
When the Hero of Chippewa took to his heels,
His "six feet five inches" fast striding the fields,
As if Brock and his British, and the Seminole
pack,
And the Mexican's "lasso" were all on his track!

Oh! never before 'midst the deadliest blows,
Had the gallant old chief turned his back to his foes,
No marvel he sped his inglorious flight
When for foes he had brethren and kinsmen in
sight!
His footsteps might well be as fleet as the wind,
Virginia! the Nemesis, followed behind!

'Tis fitting that now from his shoulder should fall—
That shoulder once pierced by the enemy's ball—
The token of honor—if happen it must,
This his epaulette's fame should be trailed in the
dust;
'Tis just retribution it be on the soil,
His native, his own, which he sought to despoil!

M. J. P.

THE LITTLE ZOUAVE.

One little stocky fellow in the Fire regiment killed thirteen men in thirteen shots. He was afterward killed himself.

'TWAS a little Zouave, of the fireman sort,
His face powder-blackened, his hair shingled
short,
His brawny chest naked, his eyes flashing flame,
As over the red field of battle he came;

Then c-r-r-rack! went his gun,
On the banks of Bull Run,
And the great rebel army was lessened by one.

The batteries thundered, the cannon-balls flew,
The smoke and the dust hid the soldiers from view;
But whenever the cloud lifted up, you might scan
The little Zouave taking aim at his man.
Then c-r-r-rack! went his gun,
On the banks of Bull Run,
And put a quietus to some rebel's fun.

The day was a scorcher, the men were athirst,
And the little Zouave often fluently cursed;
But still he pressed on among shrapnel and shell,
And each time he fired an enemy fell;
For c-r-r-rack! went his gun,
On the banks of Bull Run,
And every shot told, on the dead list, for one.

The rebels, astonished, remarked, now and then,
"Them red-legged devils fight wuss'n our men,"
For they saw that no rebel and traitor could have
One quarter the pluck of the little Zouave;
So c-r-r-rack! went his gun,
On the banks of Bull Run,
Making holes in the rascals, to let in the sun.

Still forward, bare-breasted, and spiling for fight,
The little Zouave battled well for the right;
Perhaps it was lucky he never could know
How our army received a repulse from the foe.
For c-r-r-rack! went his gun,
On the banks of Bull Run—
A Minie-ball came, and the Zouave was done!

There, prone on the field of his prowess he lay,
In the last fading light of the lingering day;
The wound in his forehead was ghastly to see,
But the little Zouave had done gloriously!
And his merciless gun,
On the shores of Bull Run,
Had settled the hash of a dozen and one!

THE LONDON TIMES' COURIER.

A BALLAD—NOT BY CAMPBELL.

A HORSEMAN, from Manassas bound,
Cries: "Soldier, noble soldier!
I'll give to thee a golden pound
To 'pass' me o'er the border."

"Now, who be ye, so *skeered* and wild,
Would cross this guarded river!"
Oh! I'm the *Thunderer's* fav'*rite* child,
Most dead to reach a *kiver*.

"Jeff Davis' horse behind pursues,
Around my *rear* they hover;
His 'Tigers,' *what* would they not do,
Should they my tracks discover?

"Ten hours before these desperate men,
I'ved spared nor spur nor leather;
For should they find me in the glen,
My blood would stain the heather."

By this the hosts came on apace—
Came bellowing, shouting, shrieking;
And as he heard, the horseman's face
Grew pale as he was speaking.

Out spoke the tardy Lincolnite:
"I'll pass you, *Doc*—I'm ready;
It is not for that *sovereign* bright,
But for your sovereign lady.

"And by my word and by my sword!
You shall no longer tarry;

I'll take you past each picket-guard,
For fear you might miscarry."

Yet still as wilder surged that flood,
And as the night grew drear'er,
The soldier at his post still stood,
Transfixed with mortal terror.

"Oh! haste thee, haste!" the horseman cries,
"Though it should rain and thunder,
I'd meet the raging of the skies,
But not Jeff Davis' anger."

The twain have left Virginia's shore,
Sad Maryland receives them;
The soldier vows that never more
Shall fanatics deceive him.

'Says *Inker*-man, with mournful smile:
"Southward no more I'll roam;
I'll steer my bark to Erin's Isle,
For Erin is my home."

P. H. D.

—*New-Orleans Picayune.*

THE HEMPEN CRAVAT.

BY R. H. STODDARD.

THE Southern costume, have you heard of it, sirs?
Is a single shirt-collar and a big pair of spurs;
'Tis airy for summer, there's no doubt of that,
But not half so neat as a hempen cravat.

To begin with the collar: suppose a long march,
In the hot, broiling sun, what becomes of the starch?
Why, it wilts down with sweat—a nasty thing that,
Which is never the case with the hempen cravat!

Their spurs may be good till a battle begins,
But won't they be likely to scratch their own shins
When they come to retreat? for they *may* come to that,
But they cannot retreat, with the hempen cravat!

O the hempen cravat is an elegant thing!
For once on your neck, it gives you full swing;
These hot Southern gentlemen ought to like that,
For they all want to swing—in the hempen cravat!

'Tis as cheap as 'tis useful, a blessing to-day,
When the South, owing millions, has nothing to pay;
So, to show our good will, (they've but little of
that,)
We'll furnish them, gratis, the hempen cravat!

We try it on Pat, when he snatches a knife,
And slithers the windpipe of mother or wife;
He was crazy with whiskey, no matter for that,
He must die like a dog in the hempen cravat!

What is Pat's little frolic to what they have done?
'Tis the foulest conspiracy under the sun;
The treason of Arnold was nothing to that,
Yet *he* richly deserved the hempen cravat!

They plotted like him, with no wrongs to repay;
How could they be wronged, when they had their
own way?
They bullied the North, we submitted to that,
And, once in a while, to the hempen cravat!

They wasted our treasure, by putting in Cobb
To shell it out freely, in other words, rob;
When the country was bankrupt—he brought us
to that—
He resigned, and ran off from the hempen cravat!

We had a few arsenals, so they employed
A traitor to empty them—Brigadier Floyd;
He sent our arms South, for this and for that,
And stripped us of all—but the hempen cravat!

Our gold in their pockets, our guns in their hands,
Of course we must listen to all their demands;
They will break up the Union—what say ye to that?
My answer, brave boys, is the hempen cravat!

By the blood of our sires, that on Bunker's old hill
Was poured out like water, (it flows in us still!)
We will crush them, or perish, (no danger of that!)
With sword, and with shot, and the hempen cravat!

Should we happen to meet with these bold pirateers,
They'll find a queer slip-knot tied under their ears,
And swift at the yard-arm—a gallus place that—
They'll dance a gay jig, in the hempen cravat!

Then work all your rope-walks, and working them,
sing,
"O the hempen cravat is a wonderful thing!"
Who can mention a better, may take my old hat,
But till then I go in for the hempen cravat!

ABOU BEN BUTLER.

ABOU BEN BUTLER (may his tribe increase!)
Awoke one night down by the old Balize,
And saw, outside the comfort of his room,
Making it warmer for the gathering gloom,
A black man shivering in the winter's cold.
Exceeding courage made Ben Butler bold,
And to the presence in the dark he said:
"What wantest thou?" The figure raised its head,
And with a look made of all sad accord,
Answered—"The men who'll serve the purpose of the Lord."
"And am I one?" said Butler. "Nay, not so,"
Replied the black man. Butler spoke more low,
But cheerly still; and said: "*As I am Ben,*
You'll not have cause to tell me that again!"

The figure bowed and vanished. The next night
It came once more, environed strong in light,
And showed the names whom love of Freedom blessed,
And lo! Ben Butler's name led all the rest.

THE MEETING ON THE BORDER.

THE civil war had just begun,
  And caused much consternation,
While O. P. Morton governed one
  Great State of this great nation,
          So it did.

Magoffin governed old Kentuck,
  And Dennison Ohio;
And no three humans had more pluck
  Than this puissant trio,
          So they hadn't.

Magoffin was the leading man;
  He telegraphed to Perry,
And writ, by post, to Dennison,
  To meet him in a hurry,
          So he did.

And Dennison and Morton, too,
  Believed they had good reason
To fear Magoffin sought to do
  Some hellish act of treason,
          So they did.

But they concluded it was best
  To do as he demanded,
So they would have a chance to test
  The question, "Is he candid?"
            So they did.

And Morton, with some trusty chaps,
  Went up to see "Meguffin;"
At six A.M. they took their traps,
  And off they went a-puffin',
            So they did.

Magoffin four A.M. did fix,
  By post and by the wire;
But when the hour had come—why nix
  Comehraus was he—Beriah,
            So he was.

And then could you have heard them swear!
  Them chaps along with Perry;
They cussed, and stamped, and pulled their hair,
  For they were angry—very,
            So they were.

And when they found that they were sold,
  And saw no chance for fighting,

They took a train that they controlled,
  And home they went a-kiting,
    So they did.

At two A.M. the scamp *did* come,
  But didn't let them know it;
And so at three they started home,
  And *when* they start, they "go it,"
    So they do.

No matter what they find to do,
  'Tis done with all their power;
What other men will do in two,
  They'll do in just one hour,
    So they will.

And now, if they could mix his "todd,"
  They'd put some pizen stuff in,
And serve their country and their God,
  By killing off "Meguffin,"
    So they would.

And serve the devil, too, as well,
  By sending him, a traitor,
To roast eternally in hell,
  As Pat would roast a tater,
    So they would.

Just give them chaps a half a chance—
  Let them but lay a hand on
A traitor, and he'll have to dance,
  With atmosphere to stand on,
          So he will.

But those who love old Uncle Sam,
  THEY love, and in their greeting
They show it, and in every palm,
  You feel the heart a-beating,
          So you do.

For patriots are brothers all—
  Alike our flag they cherish;
With it aloft, they bear the scroll,
  "Let every traitor perish,"
          So they do.

THE LOTUS PLANTER.

A LESSON FOR THE TIMES.

BY THEODORE TILTON.

A BRAHMIN on a lotus-pod
Once wrote the holy name of God.

Then planting it, he asked in prayer
For some new fruit unknown and fair.

A slave near by who bore a load,
Fell fainting on the dusty road.

The Brahmin, pitying, straightway ran
And lifted up the fallen man.

The deed scarce done, he stood aghast
At touching one beneath his caste.

"Behold," he cried, "I stand unclean;
My hands have clasped the vile and mean!"

The Lord beheld his troubled face
And wrought a miracle of grace.

The buried seed arose from earth,
And bloomed and fruited at His breath.

The stalk held up a leaf of green,
Whereon these mystic words were seen:

"FIRST, COUNT MEN ALL OF EQUAL CASTE—
THEN COUNT THYSELF THE LEAST AND LAST."

The Brahmin, with bewildered brain,
Beheld the will of God writ plain.

Transfigured, then, in sudden light,
The slave stood sacred in his sight!

Thereafter in the Brahmin's breast
Abode God's peace, and he was blest.

THE CRISIS.

BY JOHN G. WHITTIER.

THE crisis presses on us; face to face with us
it stands,
With solemn lips of question, like the Sphinx in
Egypt's sands!
This day we fashion Destiny, our web of fate we
spin;
This day for all hereafter choose we holiness or sin;
Even now from starry Gerizim, or Ebal's cloudy
crown,
We call the dews of blessing, or the bolts of curs-
ing down!

By all for which the martyrs bore their agony and
shame;
By all the warning words of truth with which the
prophets came;

By the future which awaits us; by all the hopes
which cast
Their faint and trembling beams across the blackness of the past,
And in the awful name of Him who for earth's
freedom died;
O ye people, O my brothers! let us choose the
righteous side!

So shall the Northern pioneer go joyfully on his
way,
To wed Penobscot's waters to San Francisco's
bay;
To make the rugged places smooth, and sow the
vales with grain,
And bear, with Liberty and Law, the Bible in his
train;
The mighty West shall bless the East, and sea
shall answer sea,
And mountain unto mountain call: PRAISE GOD,
FOR WE ARE FREE!

A FABLE FOR SOME PROFESSING UNIONISTS.

A MAIDEN lady kept for sport
 A tabby of the rarest sort;
She loved to see his arched back,
A tail triumphant, tipped with black;
When his stomachic flattering purr
Proved his allegiance true to her;
Which, courtier-like, he would express
By softly rubbing 'gainst her dress.
To present cat-hood from a kitten,
Oft had he dozed and watched her knitting;
And Jemima's faith, howe'er ill-founded,
In him, her favorite, was unbounded.
She loved but one thing more than tabby—
Not having husband or a baby—
It hung in palace light and airy,
Her own, her darling, sweet canary.
Jemima once came home from tea,
Horror on horrors piled! to see
The seed, which once so sprightly tinkled,
Upon the carpet all besprinkled;
And water, too, the floor bespattered,
From out the bird-cage, smashed and battered;

'Mid broken flower-pot and geranium,
There lay in death, with fractured cranium,
All specked with red his breast of yellow,
Silent and stark, the little fellow.
Fancy the maiden's dumb surprise!
What Notes and Queries in her eyes!
With tears of anguish and vexation,
She looked at Tom for explanation.
Now Tom, a lawyer of his kind,
A ready answer soon could find;
A moment more, his thoughts to rally by,
He'd clear himself on proof of *alibi;*
But taken rather by surprise,
He opened wide his opal eyes;
Th' exordium framed to turn attention,
Of former mousings he made mention;
A modest statement of his merit,
Slightly disparaged dog and ferret.
The case went on with that acumen
Oft seen in practice purely human,
For he described the lost one singing,
There by the window gently swinging;
None could replace his dear, dead brother,
E'en should his mistress buy another!
Tom spoke of music and its power
To soothe the saddest, heaviest hour—
A perfume for the soul to drink of—

And every fine thing he could think of.
Whether 'twas change from the pathetic,
Or tickling, acting like emetic,
Our cat, declaiming, like Lord Chatham,
Was choked with feathers and out spat 'em.
About to resume—" 'Tis quite enough, sir;
Your protestation is all stuff, sir!
Nor can I think that cat is truthful
WHOSE WORDS COME FORTH WITH SUCH A
MOUTHFUL."

—*Baltimore American.*

THE UNIVERSAL COTTON-GIN.

By the Author of "Cotton States."

HE journeyed all creation through,
A pedler's wagon trotting in;
A haggard man of sallow hue,
Upon his nose the goggles blue,
And in his cart a model U-
niversal nigger-cotton-gin-
niversal nigger-cotton-gin.

His seedy garb was sad to view—
Hard seemed the strait he'd gotten in;

He plainly couldn't boast a *sou*,
And meanly fared on water-gru-
el, or had swallowed whole a U-
niversal nigger-cotton-gin-
niversal nigger-cotton-gin.

To all he met—Turk, Christian, Jew—
He meekly said, "I'm not in tin;
In fact I'm in a serious stew,
And therefore offer unto you,
At half its worth, my model U-
niversal nigger-cotton-gin-
niversal nigger-cotton-gin.

"As sure as four is two and two,
It rules the world we're plotting in;
It made and ruined Yankee Doo-
dle, stuck to him like Cooper's glue,
And so to you would stick this U-
niversal nigger-cotton-gin-
niversal nigger-cotton-gin."

Now Johnny Bull the pedler knew,
And thus replied with not a grin:
"Hi loves yer 'gin' like London brew-
ed ale, but loathes the hinstitu-

tion vitch propels your model U-
niversal nigger-cotton-gin-
niversal nigger-cotton-gin.

"Hi know such coves as you a few,
And, zur, just now, hi'm not in tin;
Hi tells you vot, great Yankee Doo-
dle might hincline to put me through,
Hif hi should buy your model U-
niversal nigger-cotton-gin-
niversal nigger-cotton-gin."

Then spoke smooth Monsieur *Parlez-vous*,
Whose gilded throne was got in sin—
(As was he too, if tales are true:)
"I does not vant your model U-"
(He sounds a V for a W)
"niversal nigger-cotton-gin-
niversal nigger-cotton-gin."

"A negar in de fence I view,
Your grand machine he's rotting in;
I smells him now; he stinketh—*w-h-e-w!*
Give me a good tobacco chew,
And you may keeps your model U-
niversal nigger-cotton-gin-
niversal nigger-cotton-gin."

The pedler then sloped quickly to
  The land he was begotten in;
With woeful visage, feelings blue,
He sadly questioned what to do,
When none would buy his model U-
    niversal nigger-cotton-gin-
    niversal nigger-cotton-gin.

From out his pocket then he drew
  A rag that *blood* was clotting in;
It had a field of heavenly blue,
Was flecked with stars—the very few
That glimmered on his model U-
    niversal nigger-cotton-gin.
    niversal nigger-cotton-gin.

He gazed long on its tarnished hue,
  And mourned the fix he'd gotten in;
Then filled his eyes with contrite dew,
As in its folds his nose he blew,
And thus addressed his model U-
    niversal nigger-cotton-gin-
    niversal nigger-cotton-gin.

"Then crownless king, thy days are few;
  The world thou art forgotten in;

Ere thou dost die, thy life review,
Repent thy crimes, thy wrongs undo,
Give freedom to the dusky crew
Whose blood now stains the model U-
niversal nigger-cotton-gin-
niversal nigger-cotton-gin."

THE BRITISH LION AND THE SECESSION ASS.

A SHORT FABLE.

A LION was sitting upon his high throne,
The mantled monarch of forest and glen,
And the gleam of his diadem brightly shone,
And the roar of his might reëchoed again.

A donkey, at distance, harked to the roar,
And erecting his ears from habitual flop,
With ravishment spurred, full madly he tore
To the foot of the throne, an obeisance to drop.

" Oh! graciously deign a poor ass to permit
The tip of thy paw with his mouth to salute;
But if honor so high may not seem to be fit,
Oh! grant him at least a kiss of thy foot."

A comical smile benignantly strayed,
  As from under the purple, right royally woven,
To osculate freely the foot was displayed;
  By Manassas! ye asses, *the foot it was cloven!*

GENERAL PRICE'S PROCLAMATION.

NEOSHO, MO., Nov. 1861.

MISSOURIANS, a word or two.
  The undersigned, last June
Was called to head the Spartan few
Who sword from scabbard sternly drew,
To drive away the craven crew,
Bound by black vows to snatch from you
  Your freedom's priceless boon.

The Governor distinctly asked
  For fifty thousand men;
You heard him ask—you *must* have heard—
I know your patriot pulses stirred,
Your patriot *im*pulses concurred
In fierce resolves to hound the herd
  Back to their Northern den.

Your hearts were right—your purpose set
  To rise up there and then;
You felt the flame of holy hate,
You longed in blood your swords to sate,
Your eagerness for fight was great,
You found it difficult to wait,
  You fifty thousand men.

But notwithstanding this desire
  The enemy to drive—
This strong war-fever for the fray—
This burning for the battle-day—
Most all the fifty staid away;
The actual figure, strange to say,
  Was only about *five*.

Out of two hundred thousand males,
  A match for any foes—
Strong arms, brave hearts, and flashing eyes,
Hands raised defiant to the skies,
Spirit that conquers or that dies—
Out of the host that burned to rise,
  But five in fifty rose!

Nearly six months, you are aware,
  Have come and gone since then;

You've farmed the field and mowed the hay,
Your winter stock is stowed away,
You're ready 'gainst the rainy day:
Are you not coming now, I say
  Ye fifty thousand men?

The foe has not as yet retired;
  'Tis singular, but true;
So far from that, I'm forced to say,
From what I see, he means to stay,
Most probably till swept away;
In view of which, ye heroes, pray
  What do *you* mean to do?

Suppose the facts were otherwise,
  My fifty thousand men;
That, starting when the summons rose,
You'd leaped to feet to face the foes—
Dealt fifty thousand deadly blows—
It's not the case, but just suppose—
  How would the thing be then?

Suppose, for every man we've got,
  We had as much as ten;
Suppose we'd made th' invader flee,
And struck the tyrant to the knee,

That I'd chased *him* and not he *me* ;
It's clear as daylight—don't you see—
Ye fifty thousand men?

Missourians! Missourians!
To come to facts again.
Where is the old Missouri fire—
Courage passed down to son from sire,
Motto: " Still onward, upward, higher?"
Died out? If not, where, I inquire,
The fifty thousand men?

Look at us! we—we've done the work
Of fifty thousand men.
We formed, and fought, and fled, we few;
No bed, no coverlet, no shoe;
Waded through mud and mire for you—
Will you not come and do it too,
And, if so, mention *when?*

Numbers give strength—five's more than one
And still it's less than ten.
Numbers, increased, do greater grow;
Numbers intimidate the foe;
Numbers lay lesser numbers low;
Missourians, I'll prove it so,
With fifty thousand men.

The fact is, fellow-citizens,
No "if," nor "why," nor "when;"
I *will* have help—I cannot *wait;*
Somebody's got to save the State,
And do it quick, before too late;
You *must* turn out, at any rate,
You fifty thousand men.

Turn out! turn out, then! now's the time—
The crisis of our fate.
Mechanics, stop your wheels and saws;
Lawyers, lay down the book of laws;
Ye aspirants for office, pause;
Ye teamsters, hush your "gee, whoa, haws,"
And rush to save the State.

Come on! come on, brave spirits all!
No others need apply;
Over the arm the musket fling;
Wear all your clothes, your bedding bring;
Your extra sheets, and every thing;
Come on! and let the war-cry ring:
"To conquer or to die!"

Let but your struggles free the land,
The State your pay will fix;

Meantime don't think about the pay;
Take higher ground—look far away—
Glory's the thing for which *I* pray;
That, or a place wherein I may
  Bury my six foot six.

I'm sure you mean to come, you know;
  Oh! perfectly; but then,
As yet I find no flashing eyes;
I hear no shouts that shake the skies;
If it's a fact you mean to rise,
Why *don't* you now, why don't you *rise*,
  You fifty thousand men?

Hark! up along the mountain-side;
  Hark! down the distant glen,
What sound is this that surges past?
A war-whoop? footsteps gathering fast?
The echoes of the bugle-blast?
  Perhaps—it may be that—at last.
  Ho! fifty thousand men!

STERLING S. PRICE, Major-General Commanding.*

* See General Price's Proclamation, page 443, Docs. Vol. iii., REBELLION RECORD.

ANDREW JOHNSON, OF TENNESSEE.

THESE lines were suggested by the following newspaper paragraph: "Andrew Johnson, the man around whom the Unionists of East-Tennessee rally, has come to Washington in order that he may attend the extra session of Congress. He came by way of Cumberland Gap, where fifteen armed ruffians attempted to take his life. . . He says that his people are willing, if need be, to die by the flag of their country on the field of battle."

HIS people throng around him; place their safety in his hands,
For they know that he will rescue their terror-stricken land
From the grasp of armed traitors, who, by means of open fraud,
Gained their ill-employed power, fearing neither man nor God!

His former friends against him! The blood-hound of the South
Upon his track! Athirst for blood, with hot and parched mouth,
They wait to slay him as he stands; but loyal, firm, and true,
He stands with mien undaunted—he'll die or fight it through!

Defend him, God of Liberty! Let not foul treason wrest
The patriotic heart that throbs within his manly breast;
Defend him, God! A villain's act might plunge his cause in night,
And dim the hopes of thousands now gathering for the fight.

As dauntlessly he'll fling the starry flag upon the breeze,
How, in many a traitor's veins, the craven blood will freeze;
For the brave and loyal-hearted shall prove that they are free,
And anarchy be crushed in the State of Tennessee!

Then rally, rally round him! Stand up bravely for the right,
The people's will is stronger than the dread oppressor's might;
Our country's flag! unfurl it! Send forth the thrilling shout
Of thousands upon thousands! Put traitors to the rout!

So pure a cause should summon every brave and
upright man,
Without regard to party, to do whate'er he can
To aid the insulted people, whom traitors seek to
wrong,
And show that Truth and Justice make a Freeman's
right arm strong! W. J. G.

Allentown, Pa., August 1, 1861.

THE REASON WHY.

Among the Washington telegraphic despatches of this morning is the following:

"WHY THE FORWARD MOVEMENT IS DELAYED.

"Army officers declare that it is impossible to make a decided forward movement until more wagons have arrived. By the fifteenth of July, the builders have contracted to furnish one thousand, and it is claimed that to march with a less number is simply out of the question."

Seventy-seven days have elapsed since the nation sprang to arms at its chieftain's call, and yet those immortal geniuses whose sublime military plans we are forbidden to scrutinize are waiting for the wagon. This suggests a new version of the old song:

WAIT FOR THE WAGON.

I.

A HUNDRED thousand Northmen,
In glittering war array,
Shout, "Onward now to Richmond!
We'll brook no more delay;

Why give the traitors time and means
  To fortify the way
With stolen guns, in ambuscades?
  Oh! answer us, we pray."
    Chorus of Chieftains:
        You must wait for the wagons,
        The real army wagons,
        The fat contract wagons,
        Bought in the red-tape way.

II.

Now, if for army wagons,
  Not for compromise you wait,
Just ask them of the farmers
  Of any Union State;
And if you need ten thousand,
  Sound, strong, though second-hand,
You'll find upon the instant
  A supply for your demand.
    Chorus: No! wait for the wagons,
        The new army wagons,
        The fat contract wagons,
        Till the fifteenth of July.

III.

No swindling fat contractors
  Shall block the people's way,

Nor rebel compromisers—
'Tis treason's reckoning day.
Then shout again our war-cry,
To Richmond onward move!
We now can crush the traitors,
And that we mean to prove!
Chorus: No! wait for the wagons,
The fat contract wagons;
If red-tape so wills it,
Wait till the Judgment-day.

New-York, July 1, 1861. E. F.

NUMBER ONE.

BY H. D. SEDGWICK.

"I HAVE flung to the night my pirate flag,
It is black as the deeds I love.
My merry men! Ho! for beauty and swag,
For every foeman you seize and gag,
For every youth from life betrayed,
For the death-doing shame of every maid,
For each blue eye whose light you quench,
For every babe whose neck you wrench,
As the reddening sea you rove,

I'll pay you in cash by the bloody score,
I'll pay you as rover paid never before,
For that I bid it shall be done;
In the land of slaves I am Number One!
I am Jefferson Number One!'

At the welcome sound of the robber's cheer,
Like jackals they creep from their cave;
As the wild cat springs at the lightsome deer,
As the viper crawls the babe to smear
With venom, and strike to its tiny grave,
They come! they come! the corsairs brave!
Hear them scream with joy to think
How the cups will flow, and the canakins clink,
How they'll turn men's blood to the wine they drink,
And how their pockets will chink, will chink!
And the first thief cries: "It shall be done!
"And I'll be Pirate Number One,
"I will be Number One!'

He has filched and rigged a snake-like bark,
He has armed it with stolen guns,
Forth from the bay it swims like a shark,
Wrapped in the shroud of its kindred dark.
All things good and strong it shuns.

How slily it steers! How slowly it steals! Hark
What whisper they in their dreary lark?
"Stay! Are we right? Ay! Our letters of
marque
Are signed and sealed. All's rightly done,
They are signed by Jefferson Number One;
They are numbered Number One!"

Ho! ho! Cheerily ho!
No longer sly! No longer slow,
The snaky bark takes wing.
No longer it creeps like a slimy rat,
But it flies like a loathsome, likerish bat,
It flies like a venomous vampire, that
Sets his teeth, and sharpens his sting,
Ere he plunge his beak in the life-blood's spring.
"Ho! ho! Cheerily ho!"
The pirates cry, "Merrily, so
To our weltering feast of blood we go,
How we long for its gurgling flow!
That we dare, that shall be done,
Hurrah for the victim Number One!
Hurrah for Number One!"

"What ho! What ho! A sail on the lee!
Mind you your helm, my helmsman stout,

About with the ship, sail her fast and free.
About with the ship! About! about!
Up to the maintop, you lubberly lout;
Don't step as if you were cramped with gout,
Nor handle the ropes so dainty and soft,
Set every stitch alow and aloft!
Nearer, now! nearer, the chase appears,
Bloody boys, ready! the runaway nears!
See her there plain on the larboard bow,
Sharp must she be to weather us now.
Look to your cutlasses! Look to the gun!
We'll give her a taste of Number One,
We'll give her Number One!

"Ship ahoy! Ship ahoy! We'll have her this tack;
She'll save us a lingering chase!
Ship ahoy! Yankee dogs! Be a trifle less slack,
Down your Blackamoor Stripes and Stars!
We'll up instead the confederate bars!
Down, down with the rag! Ha! what is that crack?
What meaneth the lubber? He answereth back.

We've a fight instead of a race!
Curse the impudent Yankees! For quarter and grace
They may sue and be damned. They shall have none.
Short be their shrift from Number One,
Short shrift from Number One."

Ah! sooth said the pirate! The answer came
From the brig like an outburst of hell!
It came in a sheet of glancing flame!
In an iron sleet of deadly aim!
And with sheet and sleet, shot the burning shame
To his craven breast to learn too late
From the Yankee's arm, and the voice of Fate,
The truth which now he learns too well:
That, plot it long, and work in the dark,
And cover it over with letters of marque,
Murder is still a dangerous game!
Begin it, and two can play at the same.
At this dark game the rovers' luck
Was little to score, and less their pluck.
For the felon blows to strike they meant
When on their errand of greed they went,
The buccaneer flag instead they struck.

Those dogs of the Perry who would not run,
Have spoiled the pirate's slaughtering fun;
The tale of their prizes they have featly begun.
It heads to-day with Number One,
It heads with Number One!

In the North there frowns a darksome pile—
So darksome men call it the Tombs,
Who are guarded there, ah! seldom they smile!
But spectred thoughts of fruitless wile
And ghosts of schemes of deadly guile
Are their comrades drear in those doleful rooms,
Where Darkness and Sin spread kindred glooms.
There's water instead of wine to drink!
And chains instead of canakins clink!
And there, with those comrades drear, they think
Of a past that sears and a fate that dooms!
In a fitful sleep they fain would hide
From the phantoms that fill the world outside.
But again that answering cannon booms;
Again their souls are fevered with fear,

By victim vanquished again they hear
His dread summons ring in their throbbing ear.
They start in their dream as called by Fate!
They start and shrink! They hear the gate
Of the cell on its rusty hinges grate!
Through the portal whispers the voice they hate.
'Tis the voice of the headsman; he calls: "I wait
For the first of the pirates! The gibbet is done.
Come forth to your reckoning, Number One!
Come forth, doomed Number One!"

POIM.

ABRAM, spair the Saouth!
Tutch not a single nigger;
They'll be down in the maouth
Ef yu cut such a figger;
'Twas England's fostering hand
The niggers here that bro't;
Here, Abraham, let them stand!
Yure acks shall harm 'em not.

When but a pickaninny
  They're wurth a lot of tin;
Noaw, good as gold from Ginny,
  A fust-rate price they'd win.
The Saouth wants money orful,
  And fits us tooth and nale;
But, oh! can it be lorful
  Tu give their niggs leg bail?

Who fired rite on aour flag—
  Dragged freemen tu thare graves?
Who luvs to boast and brag
  That we shall be thare slaves?
Who cum upon aour track,
  And scatter ruin through it?
And ef we ken strike back,
  For pity's sake let's *du it!*

Yes! by aour martyred dead,
  We'll follow Abram's plan;
On tu thare soil we'll tread,
  And hit 'em where we kan!

CHARITY GRIMES.

ENGLAND AND FRANCE.

A SOUTHERNER bold to Davis came,
And said: "The South is all of a flame—
'Tis useless for us to hold the forts,
While Lincoln ships blockade our ports;
What are you doing, Lord Davis, say,
To drive these insolent ships away?"

Then Davis, eyeing the speaker askance,
Said: "We hope for ships from England and France."

Then the Southerner bold went on to say:
"Lord Davis, cannot we get our pay?
People are quarrelling, so they say,
Who shall get the bonds of the C. S. A.
Our clothes are worn, and our shoes in holes—
These are the times that try men's *soles!*"

Then Davis, eyeing the speaker askance,
Said: "We hope for money from England and France!"

Then the Southerner's voice again was heard:
"Secession has never been referred

To the people's vote at the polls," said he;
"We have no recognition at home, you see;
Lincoln says it is all sedition—
How shall we get a recognition!"

Then Davis, eyeing the speaker askance,
Said: "We hope to get it from England and
France!"

Then the Southerner bold, with flashing eyes,
Answered: "Such conduct I despise;
You put your trust in England and France,
To help you through this fantastic dance.
I've no faith in those who don't understand,
To trust for help in their own right hand.
We must be fallen low indeed,
If we stand of foreign aid in need:
Moreover, we have not the slightest chance,
Of obtaining these things from England and
France!"

"GOD BLESS ABRAHAM LINCOLN."

PLACED by a nation at the helm of State,
In troublous times—when the fierce lightnings flashed,
And deepest thunders muttered from afar;
When the whole sky was black with threat'ning storms,
And mute expectancy of coming ill,
Settled so like a pall upon brave hearts—
How nobly didst thou seize the guiding power,
Strong in the might of right and loyalty
Then while we listened to thy words of cheer,
We saw thee bare thy brow, and lift thine eyes
Unto the hills, from whence thy strength must come,
While thy lips meekly uttered: "*Pray for me.*"

Ay, as the lamp within the holy place
Did ceaseless burn, so has the incense sweet
Ascended, from ten thousand hearts for thee.
And He, the Merciful, who wearies not
Of the continued off'ring, but who says,
Upon me call in the dark hours of need,
I will deliver—*He has heard the prayer*

Awhile we doubted, and our fears prevailed.
The scales, so finely poised, we trembling
watched;
Our very pulse stood still, and at the heart
A dull and leaden pain of agony.
Till from the helm the mandate sounded forth,
"*Break every yoke, open the prison-doors,*
To every captive liberty proclaim."

Wondering we bow all reverently now,
While words of patient love rebuke our fears—
O ye of little faith! why did ye doubt!
The Planter of the ear, shall not he hear?
The mountains may remove, the hills may bow!
And like a scroll the heavens roll away!
But mine own word endureth evermore.

Ah! now from shore to shore, and from the river,
To earth's utmost bounds, goes up the cry
"*God bless our noble helmsman!*" B. M.

DAVIS'S ADDRESS.

Scots wha ha'e.

MEN who have your daughters sold,
Men whose sons have brought you gold,
For your trade in flesh be bold!
On for chains and slavery!

Now's the day, and now's the hour,
See the front of battle lower,
See approach cursed freedom's power;
Down with all but slavery!

Who'd not be a Southern knave,
Who'd not fill a traitor's grave,
Who'd not own and lash a slave,
Yankee, let him turn and flee!

Who for hell, our rights and law,
Slavery's sword will strongly draw,
Woman-whipper, stand or fa',
Brother, let him on with me!

By oppression's woes and pains,
By our sons in servile chains,
We will drain our dearest veins,
    But they shan't—they shan't be free!

Lay the vile men-freers low;
Freemen fall in every foe,
Slavery's in every blow,
    Forward! let us do or die!

Roebuck hugs us to his heart!
Tories long to take our part!
Well their Clarkson's ghost may start!
    Wilberforce must howl on high!

All the thrice-cursed crew who rant,
Freedom's friends no longer cant;
Cotton—cotton's all they went;
    That, and up with slavery!

Oh! that millions yet may groan!
Build your State on wrongs alone;
Slavery's its corner-stone;
    On! "Our Chains!" our battle-cry.

W. C. BENNETT.

Blackheath, England.

BROTHER JONATHAN AND TAXES.

I GUESS I mean to tax myself,
  In every jot and tittle,
Of all I eat and drink and wear,
  And all I chew and whittle;
In flour and sperrits, ale and wine,
  In oils and in tobackers;
In papers, gas, salt, soap, and skins,
  And meal and malt and crackers,
      Yankee Doodle, etc.

The leather that we walk upon—
  The upper and the under—
The electric fluid in the wires,
  (Guess I can't catch the thunder;)
Each passenger that takes the cars,
  Each 'bus that runs on tamrods,
Advertisements and steamboats, too
  And guns, locks, stocks, and ramrods.
      Yankee Doodle, etc.

There's not a billiard-ball shall spin,
  But into Guv'ment's pockets,

No draughts or pill cure human ill,
  Without the Guv'ment dockets;
All carriages taxed carts shall be;
  Watches go tick for taxes;
And messages shall pay—both eends—
  Who answer and who axes.
        Yankee Doodle, etc.

No banker shall shinplasters make,
  No pedler cheat the farmers,
No liquor-store shall sell its drams,
  No theatres its dramers;
No rider spring round the circus-ring,
  No bowling-alley roll up,
But shall to Guv'ment needs help bring
  The totle of the whole up.
        Yankee Doodle, etc.

WINFIELD SCOTT.

(November 1, 1861.)

NOT like the famous warriors of the world,
  Goes back to civic life our Captain now,
 Sheathing his sword that he may guide the plough
Till war's red banners be again unfurled!
Not when his country needs his arm no more,
 Quits he the field, but when she needs it most,
 Too worn and old, to head her patriot host,
And lead it on to victory as before!
Faint with the glorious wounds of Lundy's Lane,
 (Wounds half the century old!) broken with years,
  And bowed with sorrow for his weeping land,
What could he do, that would not be in vain?
 Nothing but turn, and, with a soldier's tears,
  Submit his good sword to a younger hand!

R. H. Stoddard.

HOW THEY TALK OVER THE LINE.

BY ADRIAN T. GORHAM.

"YANKEE DOODLE ran away—Dixie he
ran after,
Russell, he stood looking on, and split his sides
with laughter;
Bull Run, Bull Run, Bull Run, and candy,
Yankee-doodle, doodle-doo, and Yankee Doodle
Dandy.

"O land of freedom! where the press can't have
the right of mailing,
Because it tells to doodle-dum how Doodle got a
whaling;
God prosper well our noble queen, make sure
our Enfield rifle,
When Doodle shows his nose down East, he'll
find it is no trifle.
Bull Run, etc."

—*Canadian paper.*

REFLECTIONS ON THE ABOVE.

BULL has got his "dander riz!"—shows his na-
ture currish;
See! the lion's tail goes up with a tremendous
flourish!

Johnny grabs his oaken stick—takes a horn of
brandy;
Thinks he'd better "polish off" young Yankee
Doodle Dandy.
Bunker Hill! Bunker Hill! Freemen brave and
handy,
Gave old Bully boy a taste of Yankee Doodle
Dandy!

Johnny thinks our Ship of State is getting something rotten—
Says he'll stave her bulwarks in unless we sell
him cotton;
Johnny, Johnny, munch your "bif"—swig your
pint of brandy,
But "mind your eye," don't meddle with young
Yankee Doodle Dandy!
Bunker Hill, etc.

Johnny's had a little grudge ever since he lost on
His tea-trade speculation 'mong the patriots of
Boston;
"Now's the time," he bellows out, "when every
thing's so handy,
To pay old scores, and fix the flint of Yankee
Doodle Dandy!"
Bunker Hill, etc.

Johnny Bull, old bovine friend! count the debts
you're owing;
Think upon our corn and wheat, and quit your
warlike "blowing!"
Provincial "poick," cease your bosh about "Bull
Run and candy,"
For such as *you* are not a match for Yankee
Doodle Dandy!
Bunker Hill, etc.

THE GOVERNMENT MULE.

BY A PLAYED-OUT WARRIOR.

IN a muddy ditch, by a deep morass,
A government mule lay breathing his last;
With harness all geared he was waiting for death,
The grim driver's summons to draw his last breath.

A right hearty chap was he when enlisted,
And took his scant rations of hay unassisted,
Stood up to the rack like a patriot true,
While his body by "welting" was red, white, and
blue.

At evening ofttime, his day's labor over,
He would pensively dream of his muleage of color;
But his sweet thoughts would soon grow sour and
uncandid,
As he gazed on his "end," and the U. S. there
branded.

O Abe! why did you allow the contractor
To disfigure me thus, like a base malefactor?
You "nail" me for life—I "don't see it"—'tain't
fair;
The compact was for three years or the war.

You've "throwed on me," Abe—I'm gone up the
spout—
I get nary a furlough, and bounty's played out—
Promotion's uncertain—I work for no pay;
An't this patriotic? pray, tell me, I bray.

But now all his sighs and complainings are o'er,
And the lash of the driver shall goad him no more;
For he's "passed in his checks," has finished his
work,
And pulled his last load of "shingles" and pork.

There are none who will miss his elongated face,
Another is ready to pull in his place;

So the train will move on and the soldiers be fed,
And no tears for the government mule that is dead.

MORAL.

O my bold soger boy! though thy "hard bread" is
tough,
Thy "fat bacon" worse, and shoulder-straps rough,
Take this sweet consolation, and don't feel so cruel,
For though both are "high privates," you outrank
the mu-el.

UNCLE ABE'S CONTRACT.

BY SAM SILSBEE.

A "MIGHTY big contract" you've ta'en,
Uncle Abe,
A "mighty big contract" you've ta'en.
The Fates and the Furies, Rebellion and you
Together have rather got things in a stew;
A sort of a diabolistic ragout,
A business much larger than one ought to do,
Uncle Abe!

You'll have to get round rather spry,
Uncle Abe—
You'll have to get round rather spry;
To plant "that big foot" on the necks of these wights,
To settle the problem of rights and of mights.
The battle that order with anarchy fights,
The duties of capital, laborers' rights,
The lights and the spites and the pitiful plights
That progress has left on the days and the nights
Of the ages, on bloody and terrible flights,
Uncle Abe.
What, hey! d'ye think it a capital joke,
Or have you been "buying some pig in a poke,"
Uncle Abe?

A rather big thing, don't you think?
Uncle Abe,
A rather big thing, don't you think?
To stand by the brink, upon anarchy's verge,
To peer into chaos for light to emerge,
While Gabriel blows in your ears Time's last dirge;
To feel 'neath your feet the upheaving and surge
Of ruin, behind you the pitiless scourge
Of modern democracy, striving to urge
You down to that point whence the honest diverge,
Uncle Abe.

What, hey! now be honest and truly confess,
Rebellions are difficult things to suppress,
Uncle Abe.

The thing seems to grow on your hands,
Uncle Abe,
The thing seems to grow on your hands.
The multiplied swarms of political knaves,
The wail of the orphan o'er dead fathers' graves,
The desolate homes and the slaughter of braves,
The moan of the widow, the shriek of the slaves;
Maimed millions of paupers on pitiless paves,
Resound from the shores which the St. Lawrence laves
To the sun-blessed isles where the palmetto waves,
Uncle Abe.
What, hey! come, old fellow, and candidly say,
D'ye think the investment is likely to pay,
Uncle Abe?

A nice sort of thing is a war,
Uncle Abe,
A nice sort of thing is a war,
What splendor, what music, what glory, what pride,
What chivalry, honor—what profit beside.
Contractors and shoulder-straps charmingly glide
And the nice little pickings so gayly divide,

While patriot legions triumphantly ride
On slaughter-fields red with the blood-flowing tide,
Of fathers, and brothers, and friends side by side,
Where hell, death, and carnage insatiate cried
In glee—while grim Horror his bloody trade plied,
Uncle Abe.

You'll have a good time without doubt,
Uncle Abe,
You'll have a good time without doubt,
In squaring affairs of the world up to date.
Strike a balance with man, and with God, and with fate,
Settle questions of equity, morals, and state;
Sift rights of the small from the wrongs of the great,
Fix discount on knaves, and on fools set the rate,
Divide those who practise from traitors who prate.
You'll have to rise early and go to bed late;
Hurry up, hurry up, for the people won't wait,
Uncle Abe.
What, hey! you have rather a long row to hoe,
You'd better be up, and a-doing, you know.

No time to swap penknives just now,
Uncle Abe,
No time to swap penknives just now.

In camp or in council, wherever you go,
Is treason around you, above and below;
While traitors and demagogues rise, ebb and flow,
Confusion confounded continues to grow,
Rebellion's grim chaldron to seethe and to glow,
And heap in your pathway perdition and wo.
A very large contract you've taken, I trow,
A very long, very deep, wide "row to hoe;"
Politeness to rebels is "played out" you know;
Don't you think, Uncle Abram, you've been rather slow?
The vigorous policy now's "all the go."
Let 'em reap, let 'em garner the hell which they sow.
The Conservative Democrats hold only low,
While you hold the trumps, and the high you can show,
Then "swing for the Jack," swing him high, and the foe
May be crushed, and the Union restored at a blow, Uncle Abe.
What, hey! for the game is your own without doubt,
So wake up, old fellow, and play your hand out.

TO GEORGE D. PRENTICE.

WHERE rests the harp that once was strung,
By fair Ohio's beauteous stream,
Whose silvery chords so often sung
Of life's bright joys and love's sweet theme?
Have they no voice in these dark hours,
To wake again the silent string,
And move once more the lyric powers,
That erst for us were wont to sing?

Where rests the harp, whose gentle notes
Came wafted o'er the mountain steep,
Like some delicious strain that floats
Amid the rosy bowers of sleep?
Waiting, I list, and fondly trust,
The minstrel hand that slumbereth long,
Will rouse and shake away the dust,
And give the lyre a nation's song.

Ay, sing of love—the patriot's love;
Of Freedom and her glowing charms;
Of that dear flag that waves above
Our homes in peace—our hosts in arms;

And tell, O poet! of the stains
Which treason casts upon our name,
And how the blood that fills our veins
Must flow to hide the cursed shame.

And now, methinks, thy harp awakes.
The dust is fallen from its chords;
Sonorously its pæan breaks
Above the clang of clashing swords,
And rolls along the embattled front,
And thrills each patriot's heart alike,
And nerves us for the conflict's brunt,
And that dear cause for which we strike.

And then I feel how it were best
A voice should from Kentucky come,
Where our Great Commoner doth rest
Sweetly, within his Ashland home.
And so I know his tongue hath spoken,
And swift the brave Kentuckians fly
To heal the bonds by treason broken,
And crown the right with victory.

O loyal bard! when others quailed
Before Rebellion's bloody hand,

Thy deep devotion never failed
  Thine own betrayed and bleeding land;
While thick and fast thy wondrous pen
  Launched forth its bolts and fierce satires—
The terror of the treacherous men
  Who lit Disunion's hellish fires.

O faithful bard! how future years
  Shall glory in thy noble fame!
How grateful Freedom, through her tears,
  Shall bless thy high and lustrous name!
While 'mong her heroes, then as now,
  No prouder wreath shall e'er entwine
The statesman's head or warrior's brow,
  Than shall for ever circle thine. D. B. W.

STAMPS.

"TAXES UPON EVERY THING."

SOME years ago, in '75,
  When our forefathers were alive,
Old English George sat on his throne,
And called this country all his own,
Giving our sires, both South and North
A government the best on earth,

And keeping us, as we were, free
From all except a tax on tea;
Except—and that made all the vapor—
A stamp on every piece of paper.

But this one stamp—so ignorant are
The country farmers—lit up war,
And lost us what's of greatest worth—
A government the best on earth.

But thank the Lord, now seventy years
Have passed, and shown how weak their fears;
For we are free as wind or air,
Yet see on what we taxes bear.

Bone, brass, bridges, bristles, skin,
Candles, clothing, copper, tin,
Diamonds, donkeys, distillation,
Express-cars and meals at station,
Flax and furs and ferry-boats,
Glass and gold and skins of goats,
Hemp and hogskin, horseskin, hose,
Incomes, India-rubber shoes,
Jute and juggling pay the tax,
Kid skins too, and cobbler's wax,
Leather, lead, and legacies,
Marine engines on the seas,

Tallow-chandlers and theatres,
And the prestidigitateurs,
Railroads, horse and steam, as well,
Ships and sheepskins, rope and sail,
Tin and trumpery silvered over,
Union shrieker's rubber cover,
Varnish, plate, and knife and fork,
Willow wood and worsted work,
Eccentrics t' engrave our stamps on,
And loyal yachts to sail upon,
Such class A is—would you wist
How much they bear, go through the list.

Niggers and all, we still are free,
And pay our duties willingly.
Apothecaries, auctioneers,
Bankers, brewers of small beers,
Circus-riders, coal-cart fillers,
Dentists, doctors, and distillers,
Eating-house men, caulkers, keelers,
Hotel-keepers and horse-dealers,
Jugglers and insurance agents,
Lottery men and faro play-gents,
Manufacturers and stokers,
Patent agents and pawnbrokers,
Rectifiers, retail dealers,
Steamers, boatmen, dusty millers,

Paints and pottery, pickles, pins,
Quinces, when put up in tins,
Porter, billiards, and barytes,
Pay a tax the which not light is,
Cattle, carriages, and cassia,
Sheep and lambs, and genus ass-ia,
Cement, chocolate, and cigars,
Cotton, coffee, oils, and tars,
Cloves and coal, and deerskins dressed,
Gas and gelatine cold pressed.
So the list goes on unending,
Every known thing comprehending.
Oh! what fools were our forefathers!
O'er *one* stamp to make such pothers;
Now we see, with war and taxes,
Our dear Union stronger waxes;
Now we know that tea tastes sweetly,
When with excise labelled neatly;
Now we know that stamps will save us
From that unstamped man, Jeff Davis.

SABIN.

AN IDYL.

Dedicated to the Georgia Regiments, and others of the C.S.R. that is, the Confederate States Resurrectionists.

BY H. BEDLOW.

YOU forsooth! and valor brothers!
  You the types of knighthood's braves!
Offspring of degraded mothers—
  Suckled at the dugs of slaves.
You at Freedom's holy altars,
  Chanting your blaspheming psalm;
Candidates for loyal halters;
  Confed'rates in a monstrous sham.

Catiline's own spawn and scions,
  Daring what no manhood dares;
Gascons with the lungs of lions,
  But the speed and hearts of hares.
Apostates from the faith of sages;
  Fools! confounding wrong and right;
Rushing on the thick-bossed ægis
  Of fair Freedom's belted knight.

Swaggering braggarts, peculators!
  Swindlers of the swell-mob grade,

Fratricidal, perjured traitors!
  Heroes of an ambuscade.
Miscreants! scorn of all the nation;
  Priesthood of the gyves and lash;
Ruffians! worthier flagellation
  Than the nobler slaves you gash.

As 'gainst hell's insurgent banners,
  Ithuriel to the battle posts,
Freemen march with loud hosannas,
  Freedom lord of loyal hosts.
Some must fall in this endeavor,
  But where each sacred corse is found,
To the nation's heart for ever,
  That dear spot is holy ground.

Were you littered, whelps inhuman!
  To bay great freedom's climbing moon!
Abortions of the womb of woman!
  Dear saints in heaven! a boon, a boon
Curse me now, each foul hyena!
  Charnel burglar! ghoul or worse!
Make his leprous body leaner,
  Than a three-months buried corse.

In each joint's articulation,
  Plant an anguish fixed and sore;

Through the ducts of circulation,
  Madness and delirium pour.
In idiot frenzy let him tattle,
  How he rifled loyal graves;
Let his limbs with palsy rattle,
  Like a gibbet swinging knaves.

Pain and spasm lancinating,
  Fill his days and nights with moans;
Cramp and rack excruciating,
  Twitch his cursèd coward bones.
In foretaste of meed hereafter,
  Mock his fevered thirst with streams;
Let him hear hell's goblin laughter,
  In convulsed and nightmare dreams.

By disease's vitiation,
  Corrupt his scoundrel carcass more;
Loathsome forms of suppuration—
  Abscess, ulcer, cancerous sore.
In his own putrescence stifled;
  By a gangrene agonized;
Horrors of the graves he's rifled,
  In his own flesh—vitalized.

Let him—seeming dead—but lying
  In trance's awful consciousness,

Yield the grave its rights—undying—
  Corruption claiming its redress.
With his death-glazed sight, beholding
  All the dark funereal show;
Feeling living fibre mouldering,
  And the crawling worms also.

Let him see grim insurrection,
  (Rebellion by rebellion paid,)
Arson, pillage, fierce defection,
  Blazing homestead, murderous raid.
Or hear to merry music treading,
  Ransomed slaves, rejoicing well,
For *him!* an undersong pervading
  Mutterings of defrauded hell.

Failing this—then retribution
  Blight his hopes, disgrace his name,
Blast his roof-tree with pollution,
  Drag his household down to shame.
Let consuming hate and malice
  Gnaw his heart like vultures—then
Commend unto his lips a chalice,
  Poisoned with the scorn of men.

Skulking, (guilty fear confounding,)
  In his forests dank and grim,

Every loyal bugle sounding
  Like the judgment trump to him.
Let his last breath be, when dying,
  Miasma from his Southern bogs;
Dead! then leave his carrion lying,
  "In that last ditch"—like a dog's.

TO THE COMMANDER IN MISSOURI.

I.

THY voice, Fremont, hath broke the fatal spell!
  Now all the wizards may, with busy hand,
  Wave, to renew it, each his ancient wand,
Potent erewhile to thrall in bondage fell
The faith that in the nation's soul doth dwell;
  Potent no more for ever—we are free!
  Questioned by one heroic touch from thee,
The nation's heart rings out—as if a bell
In heaven, by some archangel smitten now,
  Did, as a signal, through the azure say:
"A damning stain from earth is washed away,
And she henceforth shall wear a whiter brow,
Joyous among the stars." And, hero, thou
  Art as a star precluding light of day.

II.

O eye, thou canst discern the light and flame!
O eagle spirit, fit for high career!
True thou continuest to thine early fame,
And art, as erst, the people's pioneer,
Across the desert teaching it to steer;
'Mid all the terrors of our time, the same
As when through mountain cloud-rack, void of fear,
Thou held'st toward lands of gold high-hearted aim.
O'er darker desert now and craggier peak,
Stormed on, alas! with a more blinding snow,
And buffeted by winds more bitter bleak,
Thine eye, thy footstep must before us go
To lands with joy of justice all aglow—
To lands of which all hopes and prophets speak.

D. A. W.

THE SOLDIER OF THE CROSS.*

DOWN from the hill where earthly dross
  Ne'er stained the sacred feet,
The veteran soldier of the Cross
  Unfurls our standard sheet!
Far from the bosom of his fold,
  Armed with his shepherd-rod,
He follows, like the patriarch old,
  The angel of his God!

Through camp and field he boldly leads
  The willing servants on,
And foremost to the battle speeds
  God's own anointed one;
Tread lightly, O unholy band!—
  This—this is "hallowed ground;"
Tread lightly—'tis our native land,
  And angels camp around!

Where once our patriot fathers trod,
  For Freedom dear as *then*,
The priestly messenger to God
  Stands forth with armèd men.

* Suggested by Bishop Polk's appointment in the rebel army.

Like the fair sun, whose glorious light,
  High in its heavenly birth,
Shines still more beautiful and bright,
  Brought nearer down to earth.

So Zion's watchman, from her gates,
  Comes forth with conquering shield,
And on the "God of armies" waits,
  'Mid camp and battle-field!
There, beautiful and bright, he stands
  Amid this martial strife,
Still pointing, with unspotted hands,
  Up to the "higher life!"

God bless him to his country wide,
  And to our soldiers bold,
Through tented camp may he abide,
  The shepherd of the fold!
God spare him to his native land,
  Untouched by earthly dross;
Still may the priestly leader stand,
  The soldier of the Cross!

—Savannah News.

ANSWER TO "MY MARYLAND."*

BY W. H. C. HOSMER.

INVADED is thy sacred soil,
Maryland!
Foes come for booty, blood, and spoil;
Remember Howard, who beat back,
At Cowpens, Tarleton's fierce attack,
A chief that feared not ruin black,
Maryland! Our Maryland!

Last signer of our glory's scroll,
Maryland!
Was Carroll, of the dauntless soul,
Maryland!
Avenge the blood by heroes shed,
When Treason trampled on the dead,
And streets of Baltimore were red,
Maryland! Our Maryland!

The land that gave the nation Key,
Maryland!
Who sang the war-song of the Free,
Maryland

* See Rebel Rhymes and Rhapsodies, page 46.

While the sun rises in the east,
And patriots throng to Freedom's feast,
Shall be our poet and high-priest,
Maryland! Our Maryland!

When aimed our cannon in the fray,
Maryland!
Remembered on the battle-day,
Maryland!
Will be immortal Ringgold's name,
And Watson, noblest son of fame—
Fell treason they would brand with shame,
Maryland! Our Maryland!

One sword-stroke for the good old flag,
Maryland!
Down with secession's shameless rag,
Maryland!
The glorious Stars and Stripes uphold,
That over Yorktown were unrolled—
Oh! march beneath that banner fold,
Maryland! Our Maryland!

The land we fight for shall not fall,
Maryland!
While blown is Union's bugle call,
Maryland!

Up from the sleep of years, and fight
While treason's banner is in sight,
And shout: "Let God maintain the right!"
Maryland! Our Maryland!

We come with banner, lance and sword,
Maryland!
To guard the soil by Wirt adored,
Maryland!
In God alone we place our trust,
Blood on our sword instead of *rust*,
Our star flag shall not trail in dust,
Maryland! Our Maryland!

Up for the conflict, one and all,
Maryland!
Earth will be darkened like a pall,
Maryland!
When black disunion's flag shall wave,
No soul to dare, no arm to save,
Above the free soil of the brave,
Maryland! Our Maryland!

Let the drums beat "to arms! to arms!"
Maryland!
Leave cottage homes, and shops, and farms,
Maryland!

Rush, as your sires to conflict rushed,
Rebellion's war-cry must he hushed,
The serpent of Secession crushed,
Maryland! Our Maryland!

"I WILL NOT FIRE UPON THAT FLAG."*

BY A. JONES, U.S.A.

"I WILL not fire upon that flag,"
So glorious and so fair;
I will not harm the hand that bears
The immortal standard there.

"I will not fire upon that flag,"
The rainbow of the skies
Hath given her glory all to thee,
And bathed thee in her dyes.

"I will not fire upon that flag,"
Streaked with the morning light,
While the vestal vault of Heaven
Lends thee her orbs of night.

* A young soldier in Beauregard's army, named Picks, of Baltimore, was shot for declaring that he would not fire on the American flag.—*Baltimore Clipper.*

That flag! its glorious Stars and Stripes
  A father's blessing bear,
And with the rustling of its folds,
  Is blent a mother's prayer.

Beneath the shadow of thy folds
  I long once more to turn,
As wings the dove its homeward flight,
  Before the impending storm.

Bright vision of my youthful days,
  Banner of heavenly dyes,
Thy radiant glories o'er me shed,
  And fix my dying eyes.

Heaven preserve that gallant flag,
  That banner of the free!
Come weal or woe, what'll betide,
"*I will not fire on thee.*"

BELLE MISSOURI.

A REPLY TO "MARYLAND, MY MARYLAND."

ARISE and join the patriot train,
Belle Missouri! My Missouri!
They shall not plead and plead in vain,
Belle Missouri! My Missouri!
The precious blood of all thy slain,
Arises from each reeking plain;
Wipe out this foul disloyal stain,
Belle Missouri! My Missouri!

Recall the field of Lexington,
Belle Missouri! My Missouri!
How Springfield blushed beneath the sun,
Belle Missouri! My Missouri!
And noble Lyon all undone,
His race of glory but begun,
And all thy freedom yet unwon,
Belle Missouri! My Missouri!

They called the craven to the trust,
Belle Missouri! My Missouri!
They laid thy glory in the dust,
Belle Missouri! My Missouri!

The helpless prey of treason's lust,
The helpless mark of treason's thrust,
Now shall thy sword in scabbard rust?
  Belle Missouri! My Missouri!

She thrills! her blood begins to burn,
  Belle Missouri! My Missouri!
She's bruised and weak, but she can turn,
  Belle Missouri! My Missouri!
So! on her forehead pale and stern,
A sign to make the traitors mourn,
Now for thy wounds a swift return,
  Belle Missouri! My Missouri!

Stretch out thy thousand loyal hands,
  Belle Missouri! My Missouri!
Send out thy thousand loyal bands,
  Belle Missouri! My Missouri!
To where the flag of Union stands,
Alone, upon the blood-wet sands,
A beacon unto distant lands,
  Belle Missouri! My Missouri!

Up with the loyal Stripes and Stars,
  Belle Missouri! My Missouri!
Down with the traitor stars and bars,
  Belle Missouri! My Missouri!

Now by the crimson crest of wars,
And liberty's appealing scars,
We'll lay the demon of these wars,
  Belle Missouri! My Missouri!

TO GENERAL G. B. McCLELLAN.

I TURN from the records of deeds in the past;
  The heroes of old seem forgotten at last—
The bright page of knighthood attracts me no more,
Though the chivalric spirit as dreamed of before,
Grows real, and sheds on my country its ray—
With that country alone can my thoughts rest to-day.

Our dear native land, in the hour of its woe—
Our dear olden flag that the false would lay low—
On the soil of the one shall *our* heroes arise,
While the folds of the other float out to the skies.
In their cause let the valor of old be outshone,
And the best of the deeds of the past be outdone.

But who may be second where Scott is the chief?
Who so gallantly work for his country's relief?

McClellan! McClellan! our hearts with a bound
Declare that in thee a fit soldier is found.
With thee for a leader, so faithful, so brave,
Our cry shall be "Onward! our country to save."

Lead on, then, O youthful commander! lead on;
It is for the *right* that our fields must be won,
With thee at our head we will do what men can,
'Tis "the man for the place" and the place for the man.
With patience we'll wait, with a cheer we will dare,
For why should we not, if McClellan be there?

God keep thee, McClellan! God keep thee and guide;
Before him the strongest are weak in their pride;
But we know he may grant to the prayer of the weak,
The victory that armies else vainly might seek;
And so in our hearts shall be ever a prayer,
While our cry shall be "Forward! McClellan is there!"

—*Boston Post*, *January*, 1862.

JONATHAN TO JOHN.

A YANKEE IDYL.

IT don't seem hardly right, John,
  When both my hands was full,
To stump me to a fight, John—
  Your cousin, tu, John Bull!
    Ole Uncle S. sez he, "I guess
      We kno it now," sez he;
    "The lion's paw is all the law,
      Accordin' to J. B.,
      Thet's fit for you an' me!"

Blood an't so cool as ink, John:
  It's likely you'd ha' wrote,
An' stopped a spell to think, John,
  Arter they'd cut your throat!
    Ole Uncle S. sez he, "I guess
      He'd skurce ha' stopped," sez he,
    "To mind his p's and q's ef that weasan'
      Hed belonged to ole J. B.,
      Instid o' you an' me!"

Ef *I* turned mad dogs loose, John,
  On *your* front-parlor stairs,

Would it jest meet your views, John,
  To wait an' sue their heirs?
    Ole Uncle S. sez he, "I guess,
      I on'y guess," sez he,
    "Thet, ef Vattel on *his* toes fell,
      'Twould kind o' rile J. B.,
      Ez wall ez you an' me!"

Who made the law thet hurts, John,
  Heads I win—ditto, tails?
"*J. B.*" was on his shirts, John,
  Onless my memory fails.
    Ole Uncle S. sez he, "I guess,
      (I'm good at thet,)" sez he,
    "Thet sauce for goose an't *jest* the juice
      For ganders with J. B.,
      No more than you or me!"

When your rights was our wrong, John,
  You didn't stop for fuss:
Britanny's trident-prongs, John,
  Was good 'nough law for us.
    Ole Uncle S. sez he, "I guess,
      Though physic's good," sez he,
    "It doesn't foller that he can swaller
      Prescriptions signed '*J. B.*,'
      Put up by you and me!"

We own the ocean, tu, John:
  You mustn't take it hard
Ef we can't think with you, John,
  It's jest your own back yard.
    Ole Uncle S. sez he, "I guess,
      Ef *thet's* his claim," sez he,
    "The fencin'-stuff'll cost enough
      To bust up friend J. B.,
      Ez wal ez you an' me!"

Why talk so dreffle big, John,
  Of honor, when it meant
You didn't care a fig, John,
  But just for *ten per cent?*
    Ole Uncle S. sez he, "I guess
      He's like the rest," sez he:
    "When all is done, it's number one
      Thet's nearest to J. B.,
      Ez wal ez you an' me!"

THE C. S. A. COMMISSIONERS.

YE jolly Yankee gentlemen, who live at home in ease,
How little do ye think upon the dangers of the seas!
The winds and waves, the whales and sharks, you've heard of long ago,
But there are things much worse than these, as presently I'll show.
If you're a true-bred Union man, go joyful where you please;
Beneath the glorious Stars and Stripes cross safe the stormy seas;
But look out for "San Jacintos" that may catch you on your way,
If you're acting as Commissioner for the noble (?) C. S. A.

And now you'll guess my subject, and what my song's about;
But I'd not have put them into rhyme, if *they* hadn't first put out;
For they *put out* of Charleston, when the night was drear and dark,
And then they put out all the lights, that they might not be a mark;

And then they did put out to sea, (though here
there seems a hitch,
For what could they expect to see when the night
was black as pitch?)
But they somehow 'scaped the Union ships, and
hoped on some fine day
To land in Europe and to "blow" about the C. S. A.

They safely got to Cuba, and landed in Havana;
Described the power and glory of New-Orleans
and Savannah;
Declared that running the blockade was a thing
by no means hard,
And boasted of the vict'ries won by their valiant
Beauregard;
Davis's skill in government could never be sur-
passed—
The amazing strokes of genius by which he cash
amassed;
Foreign bankers would acknowledge, ere a month
had passed away,
That the true financial paradise was in the C. S. A.

. . . .

Some days are passed, and pleasantly, upon Ber-
muda's Isle,
The sun is shining bright and fair, and nature
seems to smile;

The breezes waved the British flag that fluttered
o'er the "Trent,"
And the ripples rose to lave her sides, as proudly
on she went.
Mason and Slidell, on deck, thought all their dan-
gers past,
And poked each others' ribs and laughed, as they
leant against the mast:
"Haven't the Yankees just been 'done' uncom-
monly nice, eh?
"They've got most money, but the *brains* are in
the C. S. A.!"

You have heard the ancient proverb, and, though
old, it's very good,
Which hints "that it's better not to crow until
you've left the wood."
And so it proved with these two gents; for at that
moment—souse!
A cannon-shot fell splash across the steamer's
bows.
The San Jacinto came up close, and though rather
rude, 'tis true,
Good Wilkes he hailed the Trent and said, "I'll
thank you to heave to;

If you don't give up two rascals, I must blow you
right away.
Mason and Slidell they're named, and they're
from the C. S. A."

The British Captain raged and swore; but then
what could he do?
It scarcely would be worth his while to be blown
up, he knew;
Wilkes's marines, with bayonets fixed, were standing on the Trent,
So he gave up the traitors, and o'er the side they
went.
Wilkes, having got them, wished they'd feel pleasant and at home,
So offered his best cabins, if their ladies chose to
come;
But they shook their heads, and merely smiled; I
am sorry for to say,
Conjugality's at a discount down in the C. S. A.

They coolly said unto their lords: "Our dresses
all are new;
What on earth would be the use of going back
with you?

And though we're very sorry that your plans are
undone,
We mean to pass the winter in Paris and in London.
'Stead of bothering you, and sharing your prison
beds and fetters,
We'll write each mail from Europe the most delightful letters;
Tell you of all we've done and seen, at party, ball,
or play,
To cheer your hearts, poor martyrs to *cotton* and
C. S. A."

So the two vessels parted; the San Jacinto
went
To unload her precious cargo, while the captain of
the Trent,
Having lost a (probable) *douceur* which had
seemed within his grip,
We presume, for consolation, retired and took a
nip.
The ladies talked of the affair less with a tear than
smile;
Their lords and masters took their way to Warren's
Fort the while;

And gratis lodged and boarded there, they may
think for many a day
That brains are sometimes northward found as
well's in the C. S. A.

ECLOGA.

ARCADES ambo:
Et cantare pares, et respondere parati.

SCENE—Fort Warren. TIME—11 A.M., January first, 1862.

MASON—SLIDELL.

Tug Starlight approaching.

SLIDELL, LOQUITUR.

HAPPY New Year! You've got a shocking
cough,
The tug is coming, and we'll soon be off.

MASON.

That wretched craft? Am I to go in her?
That cockboat carry an ambassador!
Slidell, I own, to make a frank confession,
I've changed my early notions of secession.
Jeff talked it up—I was a fool to heed him—
And half persuaded me I might succeed him.

They've stopped our rations of champagne and
oysters.
How I detest those cursed Yankee cloisters!
The cot I sleep on's harder than a bullet;
The grub we got is sticking in my gullet.

SLIDELL.

Mason, you are right; for, argue as we may,
Our missionary labors will not pay.
As for myself, I'd freely give a guinea
If I was safely back in ole Virginny.
When last at Bunker Hill, how could you know
You'd soon be here again—a plenipo?

MASON.

Speak in a lower tone; you trifle, Slidell;
Such recreant badinage is worse than idle.
Besides, you see those Yankee rascals near us;
They'll surely print it if they overhear us,
And swear that, a short time before we parted,
Mason and Slidell both were quite downhearted.
Keep a stiff upper lip—how well things went
Until the San Jacinto stopped the Trent!

SLIDELL.

Her tompions were out—the San Jacinto,
Had we not stopped, would surely have fired into,

And possibly have sunk the British packet,
Frightened the ladies with the cursed racket,
And sent both you and me, and our despatches,
Down to the lowest pit in Davy's hatches.
'Tis plain enough we've had a wretched time on't;
There is no *reason* in't, so let us *rhyme* on't.
We've missed it, Mason—better have been loyal;
They've taken Hatteras, Beaufort, and Port
Royal;
And as for Charleston, we have lately learnt
The harbor's ruined and the city's burnt.
Our troubles thicken—let us not ignore 'em;
The Fed's, 'tis clear, will carry all before 'em.
Our troops are starving, and I should not wonder
If Jeff and Beauregard should both knock under.
The Southern masses, that have long been cheated,
And led to think the Yankees were defeated,
Know it's all gammon—all things here are quiet,
Hamlin's no nigger, and there's no bread riot;
And those who held Abe Lincoln up in terror,
A mere gorilla, are themselves in error;
As for myself, I'm almost ready now
To go to Washington and take the vow.

MASON.

Peace, Slidell, peace! our lot is full of evil;
A double traitor is the very devil.

We go to London, and when there, our course is
To draw long bows about our vast resources.
'Tis vain, except ourselves, to search all climes,
To find a bolder liar than the *Times.*
We'll COTTON to the times—it has been said
They roar the louder when they are well fed.
Gold we have none—shinplaster will not do—
Perhaps they may receive an I. O. U.,
Hereafter payable, or some such thing,
When you're prime minister and I am king;
For we must first declare our discontent
With any but a royal government,
And humbly ask Great Britain to protect us,
Receive our homage, counsel and direct us.

[*The tug off Yarmouth—gale commencing.*

SLIDELL.

Go on, my friend, I wish to hear the whole.

MASON.

I can't, unless you'll stop this devilish roll.

SLIDELL.

I think 'twill be much worse in the Rinaldo.

MASON.

If so, the Lord alone knows what I shall do.

[*The Rinaldo at sea—gale terrible—the Ambassadors and Secretaries rolling on the deck.*

FIRST SECRETARY.

Steward, I say! be quick, and bring a basin.

SLIDELL.

Two, and — O Lord! — make haste for me and Mason!

SECOND SECRETARY.

Rebellion's working upward—pray bring three.

FIRST SECRETARY.

Bring four—bring four—oh! what a horrid sea!

THE MASON AND SLIDELL CASE.

Respectfully dedicated to Mr. Bigelow, of the "Bigelow Papers."

GOIN' abroad to sell your country,
Was you, gentlemen? Do tell!
Got tripped up afore you done it—
My! '*Twas* something of a "sell."

Folks that do sich dirty business,
  Travellin' on the devil's route,
Ort to ask theirselves the question:
  "Does your mother know you're out?"

Reckon we're a *leetle* smarter
  Than they took us for afore;
Anyhow, my boys, we've nabbed 'em!
  Show 'em in an' shet the door.
'Tis n't jest the kind o' quarters
  They'd 'ave chose, I tell you what;
Never mind, they're very welcome—
  Jest as lives they'd stay as not.

Give 'em bread and water plenty,
  Maybe it 'ill bring 'em round;
'Taint the beverage they're used to,
  Where they come from, I'll be bound.
Shouldn't wonder if they're homesick;
  Folks are apt to be, but still,
They've a mighty pleasant prospect,
  Lookin' out on Bunker Hill.

Wonder ef it ever strikes 'em
  How their fathers fought an' bled,
Settin' up the glorious Union
  They're a knockin' in the head.

Reckon 't must be quite refreshin',
  Layin' wide awake o' nights,
Callin' back them grand old struggles,
  Them old Revolution fights.

Well, they say the world's progressin' ;
  May be 'tis—but an't it queer,
While old Bunker Hill is standin,'
  We should have sich doins here ?
Rebels fightin' 'gainst their country,
  Traitors crossing ocean's wave,
All to damn the blessed Union
  That their fathers died to save !

I'm not over-'cute in guessin',
  But I reckon I can tell
Pretty nigh the bone you're after,
  Messrs. Mason and Slidell.
It's "no go," depend upon it.
  You can't come it quite—cause why ?
We're as wide awake as you are ;
  Guess you'll learn it, by an' by.

Stranger, when yer suit of homespun
  With its Yankee buttons blazed,*

* Mr. M., it is said, has worn for a year or two past "a coarse suit of gray clothing, claimed to be home-spun in Virginia, as

Didn't think you'd come to this now,
  Did you? an't you some amazed?
Well, things do turn out the 'cutest,
  And, for one, I'm mighty glad
Jest to welcome ye to Boston,
  And, for two, you're mighty mad!

Never mind, my boys, we've got 'em,
  And I take it 'tis a sign
Of the blessed futur' comin',
  Only stand and toe the line.
Their "peculiar institution,"
  Knock it into *pi*, and see
What a mighty power and plucky
  Lays in those two words: "BE FREE!"

Mr. President, your pardon,
  But to me it's plaguey clear,
Ef we'd meet 'em with that weapon,
  It would settle all this 'ere.
'Tan't no use to treat 'em tender;
  Pitch right into 'em, I say,
Ef they call their black folks cattle,
  Confiscate 'em, right away.

indicative of his extreme Southern views, but which was covered all over with Connecticut buttons.

That's the talk; it's no use wastin'
Words to prove the tother side;
God Almighty's in the business,
Ef we shirk it he'll decide.
And I tell you what, my hearties,
When he takes the matter up,
Whatsoever draught we mingle,
You and I must drink the cup.

—*Salem Register.*

DEATH OF THE LINCOLN DESPOTISM.

AIR—*Root, Hog, or Die.*

'TWAS out upon 'mid ocean that the San Jacinto hailed
An English neutral vessel, while on her course she sailed;
Then sent her traitor Fairfax, to board her with his crew,
And beard the "British lion" with his "Yankee-doodle-doo."

The Yankees took her passengers, and put them
on their ship,
And swore that base secession could not give them
the slip;
But England says she'll have them, if Washington
must fall,
So Lincoln and his "nigger craft" must certainly
feel small.

Of all the "Yankee notions" that ever had their
birth,
The one of searching neutrals affords the greatest
mirth—
To the Southrons; but the Yankees will ever hate
the fame
Which gave to Wilkes and Fairfax their never-
dying name.
Throughout the North their Captain Wilkes re-
ceived his meed of praise,
For doing—in these civilized—the deeds of darker
days;
But England's guns will thunder along the Yankee
coast,
And show the abolitionists too soon they made
their boast.

Then while Old England's cannon are booming on the sea,
Our Johnson, Smith, and Beauregard, dear Maryland will free,
And Johnston in Kentucky will whip the Yankees too,
And start them to the lively tune of "Yankee-doodle-doo."
Then down at Pensacola, where the game is always "Bragg,"
The "Stars and Stripes" will be pulled down, and in the dust be dragged;
For Pickens can't withstand us when Braxton is the cry,
And there you'll see the Yankees, with their usual speed, will fly.

On the coast of Dixie's kingdom there are batteries made by Lee,
And covered up with cotton, which the Yankees want to see;
But when they go to take it, they'll find it will not do,
And start upon the "double-quick" to "Yankee-doodle-doo."
Then Evans and his cavalry will follow in their track,

And drive them in the Atlantic, or safely bring
them back,
And hold them till Abe Lincoln and all his Northern scum
Shall own our independence of "Yankee Doodledom."

—*Richmond Dispatch.*

A KONGRATELATERY POME.

To them two wuthless old traitors, Mr. Mason and Mr. Slidell—imitated from a piece writ by some pesky smart feller a spell ago, about ketchin' the two sarpents.

WELL, you've got there, Messrs. Judas!
Reached at last yer longed-for bourne;
Glad to see yer folks, I reckon!
Slidell, how's that gal o' yourn?
'Pears to me 'taint much to brag on,
Arter what you've both bin threw,
Meetin' such a cool reception—
Say, now—an't yer sumthin' bleu?

Arter all the fuss and bluster,
Arter bein' pestered so,
Trainin' round inside a prison
Till yer told to pack and go;

Don't yer feel, now, kind o' sheepish?
  An't yer 'shamed almost to death?
An't yer, now, as two big humbugs
  As the Mairmaid and Joice Heth?

S'pose yer thought that, long 'fore this time,
  With yer blusterin' ways and talk,
John Bull 'd got his clutches 'round us,
  And 'd made the eagle squawk.
My! how lucky 'twas we grabbed yer!
  C'lumby would bin nowhere now;
We'd 'a bin a pack o' wagrants,
  Glad to live most anyhow.

Seems the *Times* warn't glad to see yer—
  Says they knowed the rogues afore—
Sez they're comin' jest a purpus
  For a row, and nothin' more.
They an't wurth a mite o' notice,
  Comin' here to make a name—
Sez if they'd a bin two darkies,
  They'd a kicked up jest the same.

Glad the *Times* has got some reason—
  They've been hectorin' long enuf;
Guess they'll find, afore its over,
  Yankees *have* got pluck and stuff;

Guess they'll think, from them great victories—
  Donelson and Roanoke,
And Kentucky and Missouri--
  That rebellion's back is broke.

But you've got there—arter fashion—
  Now, what *air* yer goin' to deu ?
Goin' to coax the British lion
  For to poke his claws right threw ?
Don't now, Messrs. S. and Mason !
  P'r'aps 'twill hurt us—Oh ! now don't !
P'r'aps we'll recognize the rebels—
  Then, again, perhaps we won't !

S'pose yer think that, now yer got there,
  Every thing 'll go fust-rate ;
Ef yer wait till England helps yer,
  Kind o' think ye'll have to wait.
I'll be whipped ef I believe it,
  And I raly think it's treu
That they wouldn't come to lick us,
  Ef the queen did tell 'em to.

J. M.

A CATECHISM FOR THE TIMES.

BY M. ARY.

WHO were the men Jeff Davis sent
Aboard the English steamer Trent,
To land on Britain's shores intent?
Slidell and Mason.

What was it came athwart their way,
As they across the ocean stray,
And captured them without delay?
The San Jacinto.

Who was it bragged and talked so wise,
And told the biggest sort o' lies,
While crowds looked on with wide-stretched eyes?
Lieutenant Williams.

Who was it then began to roar,
And bellow forth from shore to shore,
Just like the bear whose head was sore?
John Bull.

What was it joined the hue and cry,
Looked o'er the sea with flashing eye,
As if whole armies to defy?
The London *Times*.

Who dared us, like some angry chap,
To touch the chip upon his cap,
And clenched his fist to give the rap?
Lord Palmerston.

Who was it for a cotton-bale
Could of its principles make sale,
And welcome traitors to its pale?
Old England.

Who was it said 'twould never do
To fight for such a rebel crew,
Unfit to earn the bread they chew?
Abe Lincoln.

(If Britain should want any more
Of just such scamps to grace her shore,
She need not threaten us with war,
For she shall have them.)

Who is it that, with powerful hand,
Will hurl secession from the land,

And cow Jeff Davis and his band?
McClellan.

What is it that, untrammelled, free,
Shall proudly wave o'er land and sea,
The beacon light of liberty?
Our banner.

A NEW SONG TO AN OLD TUNE.

JOHN BULL, Esquire, my jo John,
When we were first acquent,
You acted very much as now
You act about the Trent.
You stole my bonny sailors, John,
My bonny ships also,
You're aye the same fierce beast to me,
John Bull, Esquire, my jo!

John Bull, Esquire, my jo John,
Since we were linked together,
Full many a jolly fight, John,
We've had with one another

Now must we fight again, John?
  Then at it let us go!
And God will help the honest heart,
  John Bull, Esquire, my jo.

John Bull, Esquire, my jo John,
  A century has gone by,
Since you called me your slave, John,
  Since I at you let fly.
You want to fight it out again—
  That war of waste and woe;
You'll find me much the same old coon,
  John Bull, Esquire, my jo.

John Bull, Esquire, my jo John,
  If lying loons have told
That I have lost my pluck, John,
  And fight not as of old;
You'd better not believe it, John,
  Nor scorn your ancient foe;
For I've seen weaker days than this,
  John Bull, Esquire, my jo.

John Bull, Esquire, my jo John,
  Hear this my language plain:
I never smote you unprovoked,
  I never smote in vain.

If you want peace, peace let it be!
  If war, be pleased to know,
Shots in my locker yet remain,
  John Bull, Esquire, my jo!

TARDY GEORGE.

WHAT are you waiting for, George, I pray?
  To scour your cross-belts with fresh pipe-clay?
To burnish your buttons, to brighten your guns;
Or wait you for May-day and warm-spring suns?
Are you blowing your fingers because they are cold,
Or catching your breath ere you take a hold?
Is the mud knee-deep in valley and gorge?
What are you waiting for, tardy George?

Want you a thousand more cannon made,
To add to the thousand now arrayed?
Want you more men, more money to pay?
Are not two millions enough per day?
Wait you for gold and credit to go,
Before we shall see your martial show;

Till Treasury Notes will not pay to forge?
What are you waiting for, tardy George?

Are you waiting for your hair to turn,
Your heart to soften, your bowels to yearn
A little more toward "our Southern friends,"
As at home and abroad they work their ends?
"Our Southern friends!" whom you hold so dear
That you do no harm and give no fear,
As you tenderly take them by the gorge —
What are you waiting for, tardy George?

Now that you've marshalled your whole command,
Planned what you would, and changed what you
planned;
Practised with shot and practised with shell,
Know to a hair where every one fell,
Made signs by day and signals by night;
Was it all done to keep out of a fight?
Is the whole matter too heavy a charge?
What are you waiting for, tardy George?

Shall we have more speeches, more reviews?
Or are you waiting to hear the news;
To hold up your hands in mute surprise,
When France and England shall "recognize"?

Are you too grand to fight traitors small?
Must you have a nation to cope withal?
Well, hammer the anvil and blow the forge—
You'll soon have a dozen, tardy George.

Suppose for a moment, George, my friend—
Just for a moment—you condescend
To use the means that are in your hands,
The eager muskets and guns and brands;
Take one bold step on the Southern sod,
And leave the issue to watchful God!
For now the nation raises its gorge,
Waiting and watching you, tardy George.

I should not much wonder, George, my boy,
If Stanton get in his head a toy,
And some fine morning, ere you are out,
He send you all "to the right about"—
You and Jomini, and all the crew
Who think that war is nothing to do
But to drill and cypher, and hammer and forge—
What are you waiting for, tardy George?

January, 1862.

McCLELLAN'S SOLILOQUY.

BY A DAUGHTER OF GEORGIA.

ADVANCE or not advance; that is the question.
Whether 'tis better in the mind to suffer
The jeers and howlings of outrageous Congressmen;
Or to take up arms against a host of rebels,
And, by opposing, beat them? — To fight — to win—
No more: and by a victory, to say we end
This war, and all the thousand dreadful shocks
The flesh's exposed to—'tis a consummation
Devoutly to be wished. To fight, to win,
To beat! perchance be beaten; ay, there's the rub;
After a great defeat, what would ensue!
When we have shuffled off the battle-field,
Must give us pause; there's the respect,
That makes calamity a great defeat.
But shall I bear the scorn of all the North,
The "outward" pressure and old Abe's reviling,
The pangs of being scoffed at for this long delay,
The turning out of office, (ay, perchance,

When I myself might now my greatness make
With a great battle?) I'd not longer bear
To drill and practise troops behind intrenchments,
But that the fear of meeting with the foe
On dread Manassas, from whose plains
Few of us would return, puzzles my will,
And makes me rather bear the ills I have
Than fly to others which are greater far.
These Southerners make cowards of us all.

—*Charleston Mercury.*

OVERTURES FROM RICHMOND.

A NEW LILLIBURLERO.

BY PROFESSOR F. J. CHILD.

"WELL, Uncle Sam," says Jefferson D.,
Lilliburlero, old Uncle Sam,
"You'll have to join my Confed'racy,"
Lilliburlero, old Uncle Sam.
"Lero, lero, that don't appear O, that don't appear," says old Uncle Sam.
"Lero, lero, fillibustero, that don't appear," says old Uncle Sam."

" So, Uncle Sam, just lay down your arms,"
Lilliburlero, etc.,
" Then you shall hear my reas'nable terms,"
Lilliburlero, etc.
" Lero, lero, I'd like to hear O, I'd like to hear,"
says old Uncle Sam,
" Lero, lero, fillibustero, I'd like to hear," says old
Uncle Sam.

" First, you must own I've beat you in fight,"
Lilliburlero, etc.,
" Then, that I always have been in the right,"
Lilliburlero, etc.,
" Lero, lero, rather severe O, rather severe," says
old Uncle Sam.
" Lero, lero, fillibustero, rather severe," says old
Uncle Sam.

" Then you must pay my national debts,"
Lilliburlero, etc.,
" No questions asked about my assets,"
Lilliburlero, etc.
" Lero, lero, that's very dear O, that's very dear,"
says old Uncle Sam,
" Lero, lero, fillibustero, that's very dear, says old
Uncle Sam.

"Also, some few I.O.U'S and bets,"
Lilliburlero, etc.,
"Mine and Bob Toombs' and Sildell's and Rhett's,"
Lilliburlero, etc.
"Lero, lero, that leaves me zero, that leaves me zero," says Uncle Sam.
"Lero, lero, fillibustero, that leaves me zero," says Uncle Sam.

"And, by the way, one little thing more,"
Lilliburlero, etc.,
"You're to refund the cost of the war,"
Lilliburlero, etc.
"Lero, lero, just what I fear O, just what I fear," says old Uncle Sam,
"Lero, lero, fillibustero, just what I fear," says old Uncle Sam.

"Next, you must own our cavalier blood!"
Lilliburlero, etc.,
"And that your Puritans sprang from the mud!"
Lilliburlero, etc.
"Lero, lero, that mud is clear O, that mud is clear," says old Uncle Sam,
"Lero, lero, fillibustero, that mud is clear," says old Uncle Sam.

"Slavery's of course the chief corner-stone,"
Lilliburlero, etc.,
"Of our NEW CIV-IL-I-ZA-TION!"
Lilliburlero, etc.
"Lero, lero, that's quite sincere O, that's quite sincere," says old Uncle Sam,
"Lero, lero, fillibustero, that's quite sincere," says old Uncle Sam.

"You'll understand, my recreant tool,"
Lilliburlero, etc.,
"You're to submit, and we are to rule,"
Lilliburlero, etc.
"Lero, lero, aren't you a hero! aren't you a hero!" says Uncle Sam.
"Lero, lero, fillibustero, aren't you a hero!" says Uncle Sam.

"If to these terms you fully consent,"
Lilliburlero, etc.,
"I'll be perpetual King-President,"
Lilliburlero, etc.
"Lero, lero, take your sombrero, off to your swamps!" says old Uncle Sam,
"Lero, lero, fillibustero, cut, double-quick!" says old Uncle Sam.

ADDRESS TO JOHN BULL.

A REMINDER.

BY C. G. CHATFIELD.

DON'T you remember the time, John Bull,
  The time when our country was small,
When our army contained but a handful of men,
  And our navy was nothing at all?
And don't you remember the time, John Bull,
  You terribly wanted a fuss;
About what it didn't matter, if you could only draw
  Brother Jonathan into the muss?
So you put all your old heads together, John Bull,
  And raked up taxation and tea,
And bled all our pockets until they collapsed,
  And in return you gave us bohea.
Now don't you remember, 'bout then, John Bull,
  Not catching our weasels asleep;
We took Boston harbor for a tea-pot, you see,
  And quietly put it to steep.
We made a great pic-nic, you know, John Bull,
  And you were invited to come,
And drink to the health of your children out here,
  As well as your children at home.

And don't you remember that you said, John Bull,
 That come you most certainly should;
And in a great fury you promptly arrived,
 Not thirsting for tea, but for blood?
Blood, blood, 'twas you wanted, you know, John Bull,
 Blood, blood, just warm from the spout;
So we heaped up the red-coats on Bunker Hill's side,
 And just poured the beverage out.
Just recall to your mind, if you please, John Bull,
 The time when our sailors you stole,
Insulted our flag, imprisoned our men,
 And otherwise played the old fool.
We made a shooting-match, remember, John Bull,
 'Twas held away down in Orleans,
And while we were killing seven hundred or more,
 You were a-killing sixteen.
And don't you remember you run, John Bull,
 You scampered, all trembling with fear,
And sought out in haste your dear island home,
 And took to your beef and your beer?
You guzzled your beer, you remember, John Bull,
 Imbibed it to smother your care,
While we furnished biers for your dead where they fell,
 And kindly we buried them there.

For a long time your conduct improved, Johnny
Bull,
And fondly on this we reflect;
Your manner was very respectful toward us,
And your demeanor was very correct.
We were glad, very glad, I assure you, John Bull,
That from prudence you never once swerved,
But you seemed to acknowledge with a penitent
grace
The licking you got was deserved.
But we notice strong symptoms of late, Johnny Bull,
Symptoms portentous of wrong;
Signs that have changed our opinion of you,
And also the burden of song.
We know you're a famous old coward, John Bull,
A fame of true British renown;
You never dare strike at a powerful foe
Till somebody else gets him down.
Now you see us in trouble at home, Johnny Bull,
Our land with convulsions is torn,
You toss up your head and caper just like
A refractory steer in the corn.
Now take this advice for your good, Johnny Bull,
And keep your hoarse bellowings hushed;
Just lower your crest, and haul in your horns,
Or you'll get confoundedly thrashed.

We owe you a grudge, we confess it, John Bull,
  Nor will ever deny what we've said,
And when each instalment in turn becomes due,
  You will get it in powder and lead.

Mundy, February, 1862.

McCLELLAN.

O MASTER Genius! on whose shoulders rest
  Burdens, such as the kingliest only bear,
Thou standest now, to thy large work addressed,
With soul so calm, in patience so possessed,
'Mong all our living, great beyond compare!
Only the great are patient, they can wait:
Fools ever fret, and chafe at wise delay;
And now when flippant tongues unloose their hate,
Stand firm! to thy just purpose consecrate,
And let the envious Cascas have their day,
And die and be forgotten! They of old
So slandered him whose glories manifold
Halo the nation. Thy work is well begun
When some now speak of thee, as they of WASHINGTON.

New-York, Feb. 24, 1862. A. D. F. RANDOLPH.

JEFF DAVIS,

ON HIS ELECTION AS PRESIDENT FOR SIX YEARS.

BY "SIGMA."

SATAN was chained a thousand years,
  We learn from Revelation—
That he might not, as it appears,
  Longer "*deceive the nation.*"
'Tis hard to say, between the two,
  Which is the greater evil,
Six years of liberty, for you—
  A thousand for the devil!

'Tis passing strange, if you've no fears
Of being hanged within six years!

A hundred thousand rebels' ears
  Would not one half repay
The widows' and the orphans' tears,
  Shed for the slain to-day:
The blood of all those gallant braves,
  Whom Southern traitors slew,
Cries sternly, from their loyal graves,
  For vengeance upon you;

And if you're not prepared to die
The death of Haman, fly, Jeff, fly!

Fly, traitor, to some lonely niche,
  Far, far beyond the billow;
Thy grave an ill-constructed ditch—
  Thy sexton General Pillow.
There may you turn to rottenness,
  By mortal unannoyed,
Your ashes undisturbed, unless
  Your grave is known by Floyd.

He'll surely trouble your repose,
And come to steal your burial-clothes.

EPITAPH.

Pause for an instant, loyal reader.
Here lies Jeff, the great seceder.
Above, he always lied, you know,
And now the traitor lies below.
His bow was furnished with two strings,
He flattered crowds, and fawned on kings;
Repaid his country's care with evil,
And prayed to God, and served the devil.
The South could whip the Yankee nation,
So he proposed humiliation!

Their blessings were so everlasting,
'Twas just the time for prayer and fasting!
The record may be searched in vain,
From West-Point Benedict to Cain,
To find a more atrocious knave,
Unless in Cæsar Borgia's grave.

YE MOURNFUL SKEDADDLE

OF KING ISHAM AND HIS GODLY PARSONS FROM YE GOODLY CITY OF NASHVILLE, WITH YE KING'S GREAT VISION, AND ARMAGEDDON'S INTERPRETATION THEREOF, AND YE SPIRIT-RAPPER'S FLIGHT, AND YE GRAND CONGREGATION ON YE PUBLIC SQUARE, WITH DIVERS OTHER MATTERS LAMENTABLE TO RECORD. A VERY MOURNFUL BALLAD, WRITTEN BY JOHANNES GILPINUS, JR., O.K.; WITH SUNDRY PITHY AND EXCELLENT NOTES EXPLANATORY.

THE better part of valor is—discretion; in the which latter part I have saved my life.—SIR JOHN FALSTAFF.

Eheu, Postume, fugaces *anus* labuntur!—HORACE.
Alas! Postumus, these nimble *old women* run away!

KING ISHAM was a mighty man,
Of valor and renown;
The rebel train-bands eke he led
In Nashville's famous town.

He walked the stately halls which crown
  Her Capitolian hill,
Begirt with a Prætorian band,
  The vassals of his will.

In midnight caucus they had met,
  Himself and courtiers three,*
And, like their slaves, had bound and sold
  The men of Tennessee.

Conquered the lovely city lay;
  The flag which JACKSON bore
Waved proudly o'er her paradise
  Of groves and flowers no more.

The tattered banner CAMPBELL brought
  From Montezuma's clime,†
Waved like a troubled ghost, and mourned
  The parricidal crime.

There came a messenger one morn,
  As white as Holland sheet,

* Henry, Barrow, and Totten, the triad of traitors, who sold Tennessee to the Confederacy and their names to eternal infamy.

† The flag of Governor Campbell's "Bloody First," riddled at Monterey and Buena Vista, now hanging in the Capitol.

And cried: "The Yankee sailor, Foote,
Is coming with his fleet!"

In ran another messenger,
With swift and lengthened stride,
And said: "Two hundred thousand men
With Buell I descried!"

And yet another courier cried:
"Andrew, thy ancient foe,
Comes breathing sulphurous fire and smoke,
Like Pluto down below!"

King Isham put his dexter hand
Beneath his scrawny ham,*
And then he vowed a dreadful vow,
And clinched it with a d—n.

"Hear me, great Jeff! To-day I'll dig†
A ditch both deep and wide,
And then I'll gird my sabre on,
Which is both true and tried.

* See Genesis, chap. 24, verses 2–3. An excellent and venerable mode of taking the oath, as it was supposed to be tightened by this simple ceremony. Would it not be well for the Government to try this process on slippery rebels, especially as it has them "on the hip" already?

† Iliad, Book I. v. 37.

"And ere I run from that 'last ditch,' *
Along Sewanee's shore,
One hundred thousand Yankee hearts
Shall fill it with their gore.

"And in my vanguard's very front,
Such doughty deeds I'll do,
That great Don Quixote's ghost shall shout,
And Pantagruel's too.

"Ill spit the Hessians on my sword,
Like horseflies on a pin,
And when I strike a Yankee skull,
I'll cleave it to the chin.

"But soft! ere to this field of blood,
Like Ajax I repair,
I'll counsel briefly with my slaves,
Upon the public square.

"For on last night I had a dream, †
With sights enough to stun;

* The Nashville newspapers of 1861, *passim.*

† Nebuchadnezzar, King Isham's ancestor, also had a vision previous to going to pasture. Isham *went to grass* likewise, and will stay there while *it* "grows or water runs."

And now, though 'valor' bids me *fight*,
'Discretion' bids me *run.*" *

Straight on a bob-tailed mule he leaped,
And sallied down the streets;
"*Come, hasten to the public square!*"
He shouts to all he meets.

Now, far and wide, a headlong crowd
Obey the monarch's call;
Their footsteps sounding like the waves
Where mountain cascades brawl.

A hundred banners wave in air,
With many a fearful ban:
"*Short shrift and long rope for the neck
Of every Union man.*"

"*Cold steel and bullets for the man
Who pleads the Union cause!*"
"*Watch the white-livered wretch who stands
For Lincoln and his laws.*"

* See Falstaff's sage remarks on the comparative merits of valor and discretion.

Four Shylocks came with flags inscribed:
"*Good women, quell your fears;*
Homes free of charge we'll give the wives
Of rebel volunteers."

Lean Bolus cried: "*Ho! mudsills, arm!*
The Lincoln hordes are at us;
To arms! and if you're killed I'll bleed
Your ragged orphans gratis!"

One said: "*To all who volunteer*
To scalp the coward Yankees,
I'll be one of ten to give
Their wives two hundred—THANKEES!"

Two huntsmen wound their bugle horns,*
And shouted out in glee:
"Ho! ho! a merry chase we go,
In Eastern Tennessee!

"We'll track the 'mudsills' night and day,
O'er mountain-side and glen;
Here's fifty dollars for bloodhounds,
To hunt those Union men!"

* Messrs. Harris and McNairy, the captains of the "Bloodhound Squad."

For still those stubborn mountaineers
King Isham disobey;
Nor bribes, nor promises, nor threats,
Can bend them to his sway

For Freedom's holy Marsellaise
Their cageless eagle screams;
'Tis chanted in their sounding pines,
And by their mountain-streams.

And thus each free-born rustic deems
Himself another Tell;
But Isham, like a Gesler, goes
Their stubbornness to quell.

The minute men, those biped hounds,
Prowl likewise through the crowd;
And Vigilance Committees eke
With bloodhound scent endowed.

And if a Union wight they find
In all King Isham's coast,
A cord around his neck they wind
And hang him on a post.

Next Humphreys came, with ermine stained
By treason and by fraud—

The Southern Jeffreys, who forsook
His country and his God.

One aged man passed to and fro,
In senatorial gown,
And in his hand a *tongueless bell* *
Kept swinging up and down.

Alas! his wonted Union chime
That bellman rang no more;
He seemed, like friendless ghost, to roam
Along the Stygian shore.

For of all sad scenes here below,
It is the saddest sight
To see gray hairs and loyalty,
Long wed, to disunite.

A plumeless "eagle orator,"
Whose tongue was wondrous brave,
Chattered and smelled an old bouquet
From "Grandpa Guilford's grave."†

* The "Constitution" *without* the "enforcement of the laws." Alas! for John Bell!

† The "Eagle"—Gustavus A. Henry—screamed for office *in vain* thirty years, over "the grave of my grandfather, who

And felons from the dungeon came,
  And men of bloody hands,
Pardoned from ignominious chains,
  To join King Isham's bands.*

And thus unto the motley crowd,
  Which thronged the spacious square,
The monarch from a block begins:
  " Sad tidings fill the air.

" Abe Lincoln's Anthropophagi
  Are marching—hellish crew !—
To burn the town, deflower the maids,
  And beat them black and blue."

Whereat an ancient virgin spake:
  " O King! to save the State,
While you and other heroes fight,
  I'll yield me to my fate!

" To Dixie's cause I'll give what I
  Have kept from love and gold,

fell in the battle of Guilford, fighting for the Union," and then went to Richmond for a big salary! *Nefandum dictu.*

* For proof, see State archives of Tennessee. The infamous Kirk, captain of a guerrilla band, who was pardoned out of the dungeon where he was confined for a brutal assassination, is a noted example.

And thus with Celia I shall vie,
  And Deborah of old."

King Isham raised his voice and wept:
  "Such grit I never saw;
My antiquated feminine,
  You've pebbles in your craw.

"But haste to Armageddon's shrine,
  And bring the prophet here;
My dream he'll read with skill divine,
  And make its meaning clear.

"For he can scan the stars aright,
  Or look a millstone through,
Or tell why jaybirds bob their tails,
  Or sightless kittens mew.

"With wicked Gog and Magog's blood
  He wrote our destiny,
And squared Almighty wisdom by
  The single Rule of Three."*

Up strode the swarthy, wild-eyed seer,
  With raven locks unkempt,

* See the blasphemous work of this crazy creature.

Like one who long in monkish cell
 On fantasies had dreamt.

The prophet cried: "Old Daniel's robe
 Has dropped on me and Pitts;
Tell us the darkest mystery,
 And we can give it *fits*."

Then spoke the King: "In dreams methought
 I saw an awful sight—
Two billy-goats, in mortal fray,
 Kept butting all the night.

"Unyielding still appeared the pluck
 Of each heroic goat;
Until (mirabile!) one buck
 Jumped down the other's throat.

"And still in this prodigious dream,
 The *conqueror* was he
Who did *come out behind*—not he
 Who gulped his enemy."

The prophet blew his nose and spake:
 "I read this vision plain—

Two mighty hosts shall meet in strife,
  And myriads be slain.

" The swallowed goat, which came safe through,
  To your great consternation,
Shows that through Buell's jaws you'll slip,
  By an evacuation.

" Thus in the issue you shall show
  To wondering mankind
This paradox—that Isham 'scapes
  When he comes out behind ! "

Then Jesse, who with spirits talked,
  Cried : " Let us harmonize ;
Pluck feathers from archangels' wings,
  And mount the eternities.

And in a chariot of fire
  We'll ride the purple skies,
And hang our Southern cross upon
  The birds of Paradise ! " *

* This rhapsodic flight is a fair specimen of the speeches of this reverend rebel, a favorite orator with the Dixies in this region. His friends called him "*the Patrick Henry of the South !*"

Then said the King: "Unto my mind
'Tis clear as noonday sun,
That unto Baldwin's voice resigned,
I now must cut and run.

"Blameless I leave—you know, sweet friends,
I never sought for riches."
(Two millions of the School Fund then
He carried in his breeches.)

Now tipsy Isham—maudlin soul—
Twelve whisky-kegs had found;
And as "old rye" was getting scarce,
He hid it in the ground.

He spake unto his contraband:
"Go cart my liquor here,
Likewise the archives of the State,
In which my acts appear."

Peculiar institution said:
"You're *tight—on me*, O King!
For as your liquor fills the cart,
The archives I can't bring."

"Then fetch the tangle-foot, my boy;
For by the gods I vow,

Since rum and I have been old friends,
We'll stick together now!"

While thus he spake, a cannon's crash
Startled Sewanee's shore,
Telling unto the scattering crowd
Of strife, and fire, and gore.

Then shrieked King Isham: "Let us fly
From man-devouring Buell!"
Loud groaned McFerrin: "Now, I'd give
My—*Primer for* a *mu-el!*" *

To see each reverend traitor's grief
Had moved the stoniest heart;
Long Jesse on a Rosinante,
And Summers on a cart.

Summers, who gave mankind the great
Confederate almanac; †

* As Dr. McFerrin's name is for ever associated with the said Primer, his remark shows how anxious he must have been to skedaddle.

† Summers put up his bills for "a total eclipse, visible in the confederate States!" Positively no admission across Mason and Dixon's line, we suppose. He got Jupiter, Mars, Venus, and

His legs were now in *Cancer's sign*,
And took *the backward track!*

McTyeire next added to the *Chase**
His "charitable" legs,
While Father Abbey stirred his "e-
leemosynary" pegs.

The prophet, too, as if St. John
Had broke his seventh seal,
Now whirled his bow-legs round and round,
Like "wheels within a wheel."

While Graves, who oft in pulpit raved—
Tragedian and clown—
Now, on a roughly ambling steed,
Went bobbing up and down.†

Earth in such close juxtaposition in one of his calculations, that had it not luckily been a tremendous blunder, there would have been a horrible collision and the devil to pay last April.

* See the letter of the parson to Secretary Chase, saying that the Methodist Publishing House was "an exclusively charitable and eleemosynary concern." Well might Burns say:

"Even ministers, they hae been kenned
A rousing lie at times to vend,
And nail't with Scripture."

† This man called himself a "Landmark Baptist." He didn't stop to set up any landmarks on his route when he ran away from the Union army.

Away they dashed for neck or naught,
In valiant Isham's rear,
Like curs with tin pans to their tails,
Or herds of flying deer.

Cloaks fell, hats dropped, and wigs flew off
From many a luckless head;
All fleeter than Achilles ran,
But Isham always led.

Now let us sing: Long live the King,
The dauntless Isham G!
And when he next skedaddling goes,
May I be there to see.

MARYLAND, MY MARYLAND!

BY R. C. M'GINN.

THE public schools are scattered o'er
Maryland, my Maryland!
Diffusing wide their treasured lore,
Maryland, my Maryland!
Oh! may they rise to fall no more,
And be all other schools before,
In wisdom's never-failing store,
Maryland, my Maryland!

20

Hark to thy children's young appeal,
Maryland, my Maryland!
Our mother State, to thee we kneel,
Maryland, my Maryland!
For us, our mother, ever feel,
Thy sacred love for us reveal,
By yielding to our young appeal,
Maryland, my Maryland!

Thou wilt not let thy offspring die,
Maryland, my Maryland!
Our souls for knowledge loudly cry,
Maryland, my Maryland!
Oh! hie thee quickly, mother, hie,
To thee for help, to thee we fly,
Nor let us still neglected lie,
Maryland, my Maryland!

We hear thee in the distance call,
Maryland, my Maryland!
To statesmen, lawyers, patriots, all,
Maryland, my Maryland!
Save ye my children from the gall
Of superstition's bitter thrall,
By educating one and all,
Maryland, my Maryland!

God bless our State for what is done,
Maryland, my Maryland!
God bless her people, every one,
Maryland, my Maryland!
May freedom's bright and cheering sun,
Till moon, and star, and earth are gone,
Shine brightly down on every one,
Maryland, my Maryland!

THE SWORD-BEARER.

BY GEORGE H. BOKER.

BRAVE Morris saw the day was lost;
For nothing now remained
On the wrecked and sinking Cumberland
But to save the flag unstained.

So he swore an oath in the sight of heaven,
(If he kept it, the world can tell:)
"Before I strike to a rebel flag,
I'll sink to the gates of hell!

"Here, take my sword; 'tis in my way;
I shall trip o'er the useless steel:

For I'll meet the lot that falls to all,
With my shoulder at the wheel."

So the little negro took the sword,
And oh! with what reverent care!
Following his master step by step,
He bore it here and there.

A thought had crept through his sluggish brain,
And shone in his dusky face,
That somehow—he could not tell just how—
'Twas the sword of his trampled race.

And as Morris, great with his lion heart,
Rushed onward from gun to gun,
The little negro slid after him,
Like a shadow in the sun.

But something of pomp and of curious pride
The sable creature wore,
Which at any time but a time like that
Would have made the ship's crew roar.

Over the wounded, dying, and dead,
Like an usher of the rod,
The black page, full of his mighty trust,
With dainty caution trod.

No heed he gave to the flying ball,
  No heed to the bursting shell;
His duty was something more than life,
  And he strove to do it well.

Down, with our starry flag apeak,
  In the whirling sea we sank;
And captain and crew and the sword-bearer
  Were washed from the bloody plank.

They picked us up from the hungry waves—
  Alas! not all. And where,
Where is the faithful negro lad?
  "Back oars! avast! look there!"

We looked, and as heaven may save my soul,
  I pledge you a sailor's word,
There, fathoms deep in the sea he lay,
  Still grasping his master's sword.

We drew him out; and many an hour
  We wrought with his rigid form,
Ere the almost smothered spark of life
  By slow degrees grew warm.

The first dull glance that his eye-balls rolled
  Was down toward his shrunken hand;

And he smiled, and closed his eyes again,
  As they fell on the rescued brand.

And no one touched the sacred sword,
  Till at length, when Morris came,
The little negro stretched it out,
  With his eager eyes aflame.

And if Morris wrung the poor boy's hand,
  And his words seemed hard to speak,
And tears ran down his manly cheeks,
  What tongue shall call him weak?

JOHN BRIGHT.

STRUGGLING with treason—torn by civil war,
  We note what greetings England sends of late,
  And with what bitter words of scorn and hate
She's taught us all her friendship to abhor.
O haughty Britain! we had looked to thee
  For sympathy in this our time of need,
And may not tell how grieved we are to see
  That thou art swallowed up in selfish greed.

But we may tell how glad our hearts are made
To find one champion in all thy land,
Who lifts his voice for us, and, heart and hand,
Does brave work for us, and is not afraid.
Because, 'mid jibes and sneers, thou durst uphold the Right,
America doth love and honor thee, John Bright.

J. Hal Elliot.

HOW McCLELLAN TOOK MANASSAS.

BY OLD NAPOLEON.

HEARD ye how the bold McClellan—
He, the wether with the bell on;
He, the head of all the asses—
Heard ye how he took Manassas?

When the Anaconda plucky
Flopped its tail in old Kentucky;
When up stream the gunboats paddled,
And the thieving Floyd skedaddled,
Then the chief of all the asses
Heard the word: Go, take Manassas!

Forty brigades wait around him,
Forty blatant trumpets sound him,

As the pink of all the heroes
Since the time of fiddling Neros
"Now's the time," cry out the masses,
"Show your pluck and take Manassas!"

Contrabands come flocking to him:
"Lo! the enemy flies—pursue him!"
"No," says George, "don't start a trigger
On the word of any nigger;
Let no more of the rascals pass us,
I know all about Manassas."

When at last a prowling Yankee—
No doubt long, and lean, and lanky—
Looking out for new devices,
Took the wooden guns as prizes,
Says he: "I sweow, ere daylight passes,
I'll take a peep at famed Manassas."

Then up the trenches boldly
Marched he—they received him coldly;
Nary reb was there to stop him,
Nary Minie ball to drop him
Gathering courage, in he passes:
"Jerusalem! I've took Manassas."

Bold McClellan heard the story:
"Onward, men, to fields of glory;
Let us show the rebel foemen,
When we're READY we're not slow, men;
Wait no more for springing grasses—
Onward! onward! to Manassas!"

Baggage trains were left behind him,
In his eagerness to find them;
Upward the balloons ascended,
To see which way the rebels trended;
Thirty miles away his glasses
Swept the horizon round Manassas.

Out of sight, the foe, retreating,
Answered back no hostile greeting;
None could tell, as off he paddled,
Whitherward he had skedaddled.
Then the chief of all the asses
Cried: "Hurrah! I've got Manassas."

Future days will tell the wonder,
How the mighty Anaconda
Lay supine along the border,
With the mighty Mac to lord her;
Tell on shaft and storied brasses
How he took the famed Manassas.

Lyons, Iowa, March, 1862.

THE "MUDSILLS" READ.

BY WILLIAM ROSS WALLACE.*

I.

WHY burns so bright in Northern souls
This glorious passion for the laws?
Why flash these fierce fires from their eyes
Around the Constitution's cause?
Why did they leap like tempests forth
When, struck by foes, they saw their need?
Hark! from the *School* the answer rolls:
"THE 'MUDSILLS' READ! THE 'MUDSILLS' READ!"

* *To the Editor of the N. Y. Tribune:*

SIR: It is interesting as a matter of news, and as an evidence of the intelligence of our troops, to know that wherever our armies go, there also goes a demand for reading matter. The Stars and Stripes were no sooner raised at Port Royal, than we received orders for papers, magazines, etc. The mails that brought the accounts of our taking Nashville also brought orders from that city. The same is true of Key West, and to-day we have orders from Ship Island. Verily, the Northern "Mudsills" are queer chaps. *They will read.*

Yours, etc., ROSS & TOUSEY.

New-York, April 8, 1862.

II.

What iron strength on every lip,
  When Freedom smote, imploring calls!
How, shouting, "*Union, Virtue, God!*"
  Their sacred swords pierced treason's walls!
Why do they love their temples thus?
  Why leave their dear, sweet homes to bleed?
Hark! from the *Press* this proud reply:
"THE 'MUDSILLS' READ! THE 'MUDSILLS' READ!"

III.

When, beaten down, the rebel foe
  Look on them with imploring eye,
How quick they quench the battle-flame,
  And mingle with each shout a sigh!
Why do no hatreds fire their hearts?
  Why rainbows banish war's wild creed?
Hark! blest Religion softly breathes:
"THE 'MUDSILLS' READ! THE 'MUDSILLS' READ!"

IV.

O Flag of Stars! wave down the storm!
  O Eagle! thunder through the gloom!
O wreath of Valor, Union, Law!
  Still glow on Vernon's templed tomb!

The Constitution's mountain stands;
  Not vain old Seventy-Six's seed;
The sacred nation shall not die—
"THE 'MUDSILLS' READ! THE 'MUDSILLS' READ!"

V.

Ye peoples, fear not that your hope
  Must sink in despotism's wave;
The lightnings from God's awful eyes
  Still melt the fetters of the slave;
Soon through his universe resounds,
  "The battle's won—the earth is freed;"
Hell moans away, the heavens roll up—
"THE 'MUDSILLS' READ! THE 'MUDSILLS' READ!"

"SHODDY."

OLD Shoddy sits in his easy-chair,
  And cracks his jokes and drinks his ale,
Dumb to the shivering soldier's prayer,
  Deaf to the widows' and orphans' wail.
His coat is as warm as the fleece unshorn;
  Of the "golden fleece" he is dreaming still;

And the music that lulls him night and morn
  Is the hum-hum-hum of the shoddy-mill.

Clashing cylinders, whizzing wheels,
  Rend and ravel and tear and pick;
What can resist these hooks of steel,
  Sharp as the claws of the ancient Nick?
Cast-off mantle of millionaire,
  Pestilent vagrant's vesture chill,
Rags of miser or beggar bare,
  All are "grist" for the shoddy-mill.

Worthless waste and worn-out wool,
  Flung together a spacious *sham!*
With just enough of the "fleece" to pull
  Over the eyes of poor Uncle Sam.
Cunningly twisted through web and woof,
  Not "shirt of Nessus" such power to kill;
Look, how the prints of his hideous hoof
  Track the fiend of the shoddy-mill.

A soldier lies on the frozen ground,
  While crack his joints with aches and ails;
A "shoddy" blanket wraps him round,
  His "shoddy" garments the wind assails.
His coat is "shoddy," well "stuffed" with "flocks;"
  He dreams of the flocks on his native hill;

His feverish sense the demon mocks—
  The demon that drives the shoddy-mill.

Ay! pierce his tissues with shooting pains,
  Tear the muscles, and rend the bone,
Fire with frenzy the heart and brain;
  Old Rough-Shoddy, your work is done:
Never again shall the bugle blast
  Waken the sleeper that lies so still;
His dream of home and glory past;
  Fatal's the "work" of the shoddy-mill.

Struck by "shoddy" and not by "shells,"
  And not by shot, our brave ones fall;
Greed of gold the story tells,
  Drop the mantle and spread the pall.
Out on the vampires! out on those
  Who of our life-blood take their fill!
No *meaner* "traitor" the nation knows
  Than the greedy ghoul of the shoddy-mill!

THE LOYAL DEMOCRAT.

BY A. J. H. DUGANNE.

MOUTH not to me your Union rant,
Nor gloze mine ears with loyal cant!
Who stands this day in freedom's van,
He only is my Union man!
Who tramples Slavery's Gesler hat,
He is my loyal Democrat!

With whips, engirt by chains, too long
We strove to make our Fasces strong;
When rebel hands those fasces rend,
Must we with whips and chains still mend?
If "Democrats" can stoop to *that*,
God help me! *I'm* no Democrat!

Thank heaven! the lines are drawn this hour
'Twixt manly Right and despot Power;
Who scowls in Freedom's pathway now
Bears "tyrant" stamped upon his brow;
Who skulks aloof or shirks his part
Hath "slave" imprinted in his heart.

In vain of "Equal Rights" ye prate,
Who fawn like dogs at Slavery's gate,
Beyond the slave each slave-whip smites,
And codes for blacks are laws for whites;
The chains that negro limbs encoil
Reach and enslave each child of toil!

O Northern men! when will ye learn
'Tis labor that these tyrants spurn?
'Tis not the blood or skin they brand,
But every poor man's toil-worn hand;
And ye who serve them—knowing this—
Deserve the slave-lash that ye kiss!

While Northern blood remembrance craves
From twice ten thousand Southern graves,
Shall freeborn hearts—beneath the turf—
Lie always crushed by tramp of serf,
And pilgrims, at those graves, some day,
By Slavery's hounds be driven away?

The green grass in the churchyard waves—
The good corn grows o'er battle-graves;
But, oh! from crimson seeds now sown,
What crops—what harvest—shall be grown?

On Shiloh's plain—on Roanoke's sod—
What fruits shall spring from blood, O God?

Spring-time is here! The past now sleeps—
The present sows—the future reaps!
Who plants good seed in Freedom's span
He only is my Union man!
Who treads the weeds of Slavery flat,
He is my loyal Democrat!

May 23, 1862.

YE BALLADE OF MANS. LOVELL.

MANS. LOVELL he mounted his general's steed,
All on the New-Orleans levee;
And he heard the guns of old Cockee But-ler,
A-sounding all over the sea—sea—sea—
A-sounding all over the sea!

"Oh! what shall I do?" Mans. Lovell he said—
"Oh! what shall I do?" said he;

"For this Butler's an old Massachusetts man,
And he'll hang up a traitor like me—me—me—
He'll hang up a traitor like me!"

Mans. Lovell he called for a brandy cock-tail,
And galloped from off the levee;
And he vamosed New-Orleans, betwixt two days,
As fast as his steed could flee—flee—flee—
As fast as his steed could flee!

O Mansfield Lovell! you left New-York,
A rebel and traitor to be;
But if ever you're caught by Cockee But-ler,
Look out for your precious bod-ee—dee—dee—
Look out for your precious bod-ee!

THE GALLANT FIGHTING "JOE."

BY JAMES STEVENSON.

FROM Yorktown on the fourth of May,*
The rebels did skedaddle,
And to pursue them on their way
Brave Hooker took his saddle.

* 1862.

"I'll lead you on, brave boys," he said,
"Where danger points the way;"
And drawing forth his shining blade,
"Move onward!" he did say.

Chorus.

Then we'll shout hurrah for Hooker, boys,
The gallant fighting Joe;
We'll follow him with heart and hand,
Wherever he does go.

"Forward, march!" then was the word
That passed from front to rear,
When all the men with one accord
Gave a loud and hearty cheer.
And then with Hooker at our head,
We marched in order good,
Till darkness all around us spread,
When we lay down in the woods.

Early next morn by break of day,
The rain in torrents fell;
"This day," brave Hooker he did say,
"Your valor it will tell.
Williamsburgh is very near,
Be steady every man,

Let every heart be filled with cheer,
  And I will take the van."

The gallant Massachusetts men
  Fought well and nobly, too,
As did the boys from good old Penn.,
  And Jersey, ever true,
And Sickles' men like lions brave,
  Their courage did display,
For gallantly they did behave
  On the battle-field that day.

The men from Mass. and good old Penn
  That morn the fight began,
And like true, noble-hearted men,
  Most nobly they did stand.
When Jersey's sons, the bold, the brave,
  Not fearing lead nor steel,
Their gallant comrades for to save,
  Dashed boldly to the field.

By every means the rebels sought
  To stand the Jersey's fire,
But soon for them it was too hot,
  And they quickly did retire.

But getting reënforced again
  With numbers very great,
The gallant band of Jerseymen
  Were forced for to retreat.

"Now, Sickles' men," Hooker did say,
  "Move out to the advance;
If you your courage would display,
  Now you have got a chance.
The foe have forced us to give way,
  They number six to one,
But still, my lads, we'll gain the day,
  And I will lead you on."

Excelsior then the foremost stood,
  Not knowing dread nor fear,
And met the rebels in the woods,
  With a loud and hearty cheer.
Volley after volley flew,
  Like hail the balls did fly,
And Hooker cried: "My heroes true,
  We'll conquer or we'll die."

Our ammunition being gone,
  Brave Hooker then did say:

"Reënforcements fast are coming on,
My lads, do not give way.
Keep good your ground, our only chance
Is t' remain upon the field,
And if the rebels dare advance,
We'll meet them with the steel."

'Twas then brave Kearny did appear,
Who ne'er to foe would yield,
To him we gave a hearty cheer,
As he rushed on the field.
"Now, charge! my lads," then Hooker cried,
"Our work will soon be done,
For with brave Kearny by our side,
The rebels we'll make run."

And since that time we all do know
The battles he hath won;
He beat the rebels at Bristow,
And chased them to Bull Run;
And had we a few more loyal men
Like the gallant fighting "Joe,"
The war would soon be at an end,
Then home we all would go,

Singing, hurrah, hurrah, for Hooker's boys,
  The gallant Fighting Joe,
We'll follow him with heart and hand,
  Wherever he does go.

THE BLOWING UP OF THE MERRIMAC.

BY AN OLD WOMAN OUT OF BREATH.

MY goodness—gracious! *Is* that fearful—thing—
  Bu'sted? How inexpressible—I feel!
Blowed up—and *sunk?* Well, I declare to man—
  'Tis enough—to make a feelin' woman—reel!

My patience!—how I've—lied awake o' nights;
  O dear!—my breath's all gone!—a-thinkin' on't!
I thought of movin' straight to cousin Joe's—
  In Huckleberry county—in Vermont.

They said New-York wasn't safe!—if that thing come!
  Nothin' cud stop it!—O my! how I dew talk!
'Twould set us all afire!—them shells 'd throw
  Every body's things—out on the walk!

O dear!—I've heerd my father tell—how things—
Oh! where's my fan?—I shall sink to the ground!
They didn't hev, in—Revolution times—
No murderin' iron things—a-steaming round!

They fit with guns—and other Christian—things—
Like Decatur—Perry—and that air Paul Jones!
No Merrimac—and Monitor things—went round
A-givin' folks—the agur in their—bones!

My patience!—I'm so glad that—thing's blow'd up!
Nothing has made me narvous—but that one thing!
I hope they'll keep to Christian—warfare, now;
For reg'lar sleep's so ne'ssary—in the spring.

JUBILATE!

JULY FOURTH, 1862.

THE clouds are breaking, breaking, thank God, are breaking,
Our foes are quaking, quaking, ah! yes! are quaking—
The war is almost o'er.

A voice is speaking, speaking, thank God! is speaking,
It peace is seeking, seeking, ah! yes, is seeking,
And cries: No more! no more!

Their hearts are turning, turning, thank God! are turning,
With deep shame burning, burning, ah! yes, are burning
To see their country so.
At last they're learning, learning, ah! yes, are learning,
To them returning, yes, thank God! returning,
She'll grant surcease from woe.

No more the cannon's roar, oh! thank God! no more
Be heard along our shore, not for evermore,
And blood no more be shed.
The deadly iron hail, the lone widow's wail,
Our ears no more assail, thank God! no more assail,
Our fields no longer red.

Our fathers' God, to thee! we cry alone to thee;
Our country keep thou free, in all its majesty,
Do thou its life renew!

These stripes of red upon its wide-spread field of
white,
This cherished blue—do thou them all in one unite,
Thy bow of promise true.

THREE HUNDRED THOUSAND MORE.

WE are coming, Father Abra'am, three hundred thousand more,
From Mississippi's winding stream and from New-England's shore;
We leave our ploughs and workshops, our wives and children dear,
With hearts too full for utterance, with but a silent tear;
We dare not look behind us, but steadfastly before—
We are coming, Father Abra'am—three hundred thousand more!

If you look across the hill-tops that meet the Northern sky,
Long moving lines of rising dust your vision may descry;

And now the wind an instant tears the cloudy veil aside,
And floats aloft our spangled flag in glory and in pride;
And bayonets in the sunlight gleam, and bands brave music pour—
We are coming, Father Abra'am—three hundred thousand more!

If you look all up our valleys, where the growing harvests shine,
You may see our sturdy farmer-boys fast forming into line;
And children from their mother's knees are pulling at the weeds,
And learning how to reap and sow, against their country's needs;
And a farewell group stands weeping at every cottage-door;
We are coming, Father Abra'am—three hundred thousand more!

You have called us, and we're coming, by Richmond's bloody tide,
To lay us down, for freedom's sake, our brothers' bones beside;

Or from foul treason's savage grasp to wrench the murderous blade,
And in the face of foreign foes its fragments to parade.
Six hundred thousand loyal men and true have gone before—
We are coming, Father Abra'am—three hundred thousand more!

SONG OF THE HOOSIERS.

DEDICATED TO GOV. MORTON.

WE are coming, Father Abraham, thirty thousand more,
From the prairies of the Wabash, from Ohio's vine-clad shore,
From the battle-grounds of Harrison, St. Clair and gallant Wayne,
With our Star-Spangled Banner waving gayly o'er the plain.

We are coming from the workshop, the office, and plough,
We've turned our faces from our homes, we are our country's now;

The foeman knows our banner, and his face is
blenched with fear,
As his scout repeats with quivering lips, "Indian
ians are near."

Thrice twenty thousand freemen, with eagle eye
and heart,
Are in the field before us, and have borne a noble
part;
And here's thirty thousand more—list the thunder
of their tread,
As they come to greet the living and avenge the
honored dead.

As the tempest sweeps the forest, as the lightning
rends the oak,
So sweep our legions o'er the field, so falls our
sabre-stroke,
With Wallace, Morris, Burnside, and impetuous
Milroy,
And a hundred hero-leaders, each one a "Hoosier
boy."

Rich Mountain's side and Carrick's Ford a bloody
tale can tell,
Where shell and shot and bayonet rung many a
traitor's knell,

At Donelson and Shiloh resistless was the throng
Of volunteers and veterans that rolled our tide along.

Jeff Davis says we're "cowards," but another tune he'll sing,
As did his traitor legions at Pea Ridge and Mill Spring;
At Malvern Hill and Baton Rouge and Slaughter Mountain's wood,
We threw the falsehood in their teeth, and its record drowned in blood.

We are coming, Father Abraham, the sons of glorious sires,
Who have heard Tecumseh's war-whoop and seen his midnight fires;
Who made for us the noblest land that patriot ever trod,
And consecrated it to us, to liberty, and God.

Washington, August 24, 1862. W. T. DENNIS.

FATHER ABRAHAM'S REPLY.

BY THE AUTHOR OF "SYBELLE."

I WELCOME you, my gallant boys, from Maine's resounding shore,
From far New-England's granite hills I see your legions pour,
From Massachusetts' fertile vales, from old Vermont they come;
Connecticut wheels into line at the rolling of the drum,
And little Rhody springs to arms, like David in his might,
Upon rebellion's giant front to strike one blow for right,
One blow for right, my hero boys, for right and Uncle Sam,
Strike, and receive the blessing of the God of Abraham.

I see from all her boundaries the glorious Empire State
A countless host is sending forth, with freemen's hopes elate;

From Delaware there comes a gleam of white and
crimson bars,
Where faithful hands are holding up the banner
of the stars;
New-Jersey answers to the call as if along her shore
Each grain of sand had said: "We come, three
hundred thousand more;
We come to strike for liberty, for right and Uncle
Sam,
Who gives us all the blessings of the God of Abra-
ham."

And Pennsylvania, keystone of this glorious Union
arch,
Is sounding through her thousand caves the thrill-
ing order, "March!"
I see her dusky sons come forth from every dark-
ened mine,
And, like the clouds along her hills, swift forming
into line;
Their eyes have such a fiery gleam, from glowing
forges caught,
Their arms such strength, as if they were of iron
sinews wrought;
I think when on Secession's head they strike for
Uncle Sam,
Each blow will fall like vengeance from the God
of Abraham.

I see adown our Western vales your legions pour, my boys,
From the Buckeye, Indiana, and my own loved Illinois;
And Iowa, and Michigan, and Minnesota too,
And far Wisconsin's prairies send their heroes tried and true.
Come on, O living avalanche! break into floods of light,
And roll your waves of truth along Secession's shores of night,
Drown out rebellion, as of old, and then with Uncle Sam,
Safe in the Ark of State we'll praise the God of Abraham.

ILLINOIS' RESPONSE.

WE'RE coming, honored President,
We're coming at your call;
Our hearts are beating strong and high—
We're Illinoisians, all.
From Northern lake and Southern stream
And Mississippi's shore,

We're coming with our quota of
  "Six hundred thousand more."

We're coming, and we know your cheek
  Will glow with honest pride,
When you see our spangled banner float
  Our sister States beside.
At Henry and at Donelson,
  And Shiloh's bloody field,
We've proved how brave a loyal sword
  Our noble State can wield.

We're coming, for we trace the lines
  Of care upon your brow,
And silver hairs are twining fast
  Your "crown of glory" now.
We know that near your burdened heart
  Our bleeding country lies;
We come with freedom's stalwart arm,
  To meet her enemies.

We leave behind us all our hearts
  Have prized and loved below,
And mothers, wives, and sisters dear
  Have bravely bid us go.

We're coming from the Southern shore
  And from the Northern line,
And humbly ask thee not to bid
  Us bow at Slavery's shrine.

We hear a voice whose thunder tones
  Are echoing wide and far,
Above the tramp of marshalled hosts,
  The din and strife of war
We hear it in the orphan's wail,
  And in the widow's woe,
And from the great Shekinah's throne:
  "Let ye the people go."

Oh! heed it, noble President,
  And nations yet will bring,
And at your honored feet will lay
  A richer offering
Than ever decked a conqueror's brow,
  Or graced a monarch's throne—
A grateful country waits to greet
  Her second Washington. S. B. H.

Rockford, Ill.

THE PROCLAMATION.

(SEPTEMBER 22, 1862.)

NOW who has done the greatest deed
  Which history has ever known,
And who, in Freedom's direst need,
  Became her bravest champion?
Who a whole continent set free?
  Who killed the curse and broke the ban
Which made a lie of liberty?
  You—Father Abraham—you're the man!

The deed is done. Millions have yearned
  To see the spear of Freedom cast;
The dragon writhed, and roared, and burned—
  You've smote him full and square at last.
O great and true! You do not know,
  You cannot tell, you cannot feel
How far through time your name must go,
Honored by all men, high or low,
  Wherever Freedom's votaries kneel.

This wide world talks in many a tongue—
  This world boasts many a noble State;
In *all* your praises will be sung,
  In all the great will call you great.

Freedom! Where'er that word is known
  On silent shore, by sounding sea,
'Mid millions, or in deserts lone,
  Your noble name shall ever be

The word is out—the deed is done!
  Let no one carp, or dread delay;
When such a steed is fairly on,
  Fate never fails to find a way.
Hurrah! hurrah! the track is clear,
  We know your policy and plan;
We'll stand by you through every year—
  Now, Father Abraham, you're our man

THE PRESIDENT'S PROCLAMATION.

JOHN BROWN SONG.

BY EDNA DEAN PROCTOR.

JOHN BROWN died on a scaffold for the slave;
Dark was the hour when we dug his hallowed grave;

Now God avenges the life he gladly gave.
Freedom reigns to-day!
Glory, glory hallelujah!
Glory, glory hallelujah!
Glory, glory hallelujah!
Freedom reigns to-day!

John Brown sowed and his harvesters are we;
Honor to him who has made the bondmen free!
Loved evermore shall our noble Ruler be—
Freedom reigns to-day!
Glory, etc.

John Brown's body lies mouldering in the grave!
Bright, o'er the sod, let the starry banner wave;
Lo! for the millions he perilled all to save—
Freedom reigns to-day!
Glory, etc.

John Brown lives—we are gaining on our foes—
Right shall be victor whatever may oppose—
Fresh, through the darkness, the wind of morning
blows—
Freedom reigns to-day!
Glory, etc.

John Brown's soul through the world is marching
on;
Hail to the hour when oppression shall be gone!
All men will sing, in the better age's dawn,
Freedom reigns to-day!
Glory, etc.

John Brown dwells where the battle-strife is o'er;
Hate cannot harm him nor sorrow stir him more;
Earth will remember the crown of thorns he wore—
Freedom reigns to-day!
Glory, etc.

John Brown's body lies mouldering in the grave;
John Brown lives in the triumphs of the brave;
John Brown's soul not a higher joy can crave—
Freedom reigns to-day!
Glory, glory hallelujah!
Glory, glory hallelujah!
Glory, glory hallelujah!
Freedom reigns to-day!

A THANKSGIVING RAILROAD BALLAD FOR 1863.

BY E. PLURIBUS UNUM, ESQ.

IT was a sturdy engineer,
The Union train had he,
But slippery tracks and heavy grades,
In eighteen sixty-three.

He wiped the sweat from off his brow:
"These drivin' wheels will do,
A better ingine never ran,
She's bound to put us through.

"Ho! Fireman, Fireman Chase, I mean,
Down in the tender there!
We've used a powerful sight of wood,
How much have we to spare?"

"Oh!" out then spoke that fireman bold,
"We've wood and water still;
Old Legal Tender holds enough
To make what steam you will."

"Ho! Seward, ho!—conductor yet,
  In spite of all the row—
That Frenchman and that Englishman,
  How fare these worthies now?"

"Quite enough, these blustering coves,
  That carried it so high;
A great big Russian up and blazed
  The Frenchman in the eye.

"His friend John Bull did not 'pitch in,'
  He drew it very mild,
And sat him in the corner down,
  Submissive as a child."

"Two stations back, conductor say,
  What made that heavy strain?
It felt to me as though you had
  Hitched on an extra train."

"Confound that rascal Copperhead,
  And all his brood of snakes!
Just at the heaviest of the grade
  They put on all the brakes!"

The old wheel-tapper goes his round,
  While waits the engineer,

Tink, tink, tink, tink! the tested wheel,
  Sound music in his ear.

"I thought as how some wheels were cracked,
  But nary one I find,
All right, save that old Jersey one,
  And that we needn't mind.

"Ha! here's a telegram from Grant,
  The news, he says, is prime,
All clear along the track once more,
  We'll yet be in on time."

. . . . .

The bell now rings, the whistle blows,
  The signal given, "All right;"
On thunders now the Union train,
  On streams its flag of light,
Which, like the beacon on the main,
  Flings hope athwart the night.
      Halloo!
The grand old iron train
  Has swept clean out of sight.

"WAITS AND WATCHES OVER THE BORDER."

BY J. B. QUINBY.

CLEM Laird Val., the great "convicted,"
Who to treason is addicted,
And who boasts that he has never given a vote for man or dollar
To sustain the war for Union—
'Gainst the hordes of foul disunion—
Waits and watches for disorder—"waits and watches over the border."

Thus saith Maury, the declaimer,
Maury, freedom's base defamer—
Pirate Maury, the Union pauper, renegade, ungrateful traitor,
Of his sympathizing brother,
Clem Vallandigham, no other,
Who now waits just over the border—"waits and watches over the border."

Yes, Vallandigham, the "banished,"
From Ohio quickly vanished,
Left, methinks, in double-quick order, to fulfil the President's order;

Being convicted of high treason,
This he deemed sufficient reason,
And he now awaits Jeff's order—"waits and watches over the border."

Pledged, so saith this rebel Southerner,
That, if he's elected Governor
Of this State, the third in order in the Union, he'll reward her
By a cowardly position,
By a base and mean submission
To his rebel master's order, for which he's watching over the border.

Pledged to array against the nation
Our State, so grand in its relation
To our Government and Union—and dissolve her proud communion
With her sister States now fighting
'Gainst secession—which is blighting
Our fair land with woe and sadness—prompted by foul traitors' madness.

While his country's in such danger—
And of which he's not a stranger—
This base copperhead and traitor seeks to thwart her every action,

And her enemies doth cherish;
All unmoved, though country perish;
And this vile calumniator heads a Northern rebel faction.

When our armies are triumphant,
Then they show their spite malignant;
And with rage are almost choking, while for peace they're ever croaking.
Democratic, a misnomer;
Hellocratic is more proper,
For, infernal and provoking, fiends of darkness they're invoking.

There, beneath the British lion
Sits this Democratic scion,
Sworn to make Secessia broader by his sections four in order;
But the people *know* the traitor—
Know this treason instigator—
So let him be engrafted yonder, where he's watching over the border.

Yes, my Democratic neighbor,
'Tis a warfare 'gainst free labor;
Waged by capital unfeeling, which your liberty is stealing;

This foul treason and disunion,
Fruit of tyrants in communion,
To the sword is now appealing, and its hideous face revealing.

Then can peace restore the Union?
Peace e'er cure this foul disunion?
No; through *war* alone can order be restored within your border;
War, till treason you shall vanquish;
War, till slavery shall evanish;
Then with freedom stronger, broader, peace will reign within your border.

Then let freemen ever battle,
And with tyrants bravely grapple,
Till each throne on earth shall crumble, slavery cease, all tyrants perish!
Then, free governments arising,
With a majesty surprising,
All God's children, freedom blessing, justice, right, and truth they'll cherish.

"PEACE."

ONE night a worthless, stealing scamp
Broke through my bolted doors,
And laid his thievish wicked hands
Upon my precious stores.

He searched the house in all its parts,
He rummaged all the closets—
He stole my silver and my gold,
And all my choice deposits.

And when I waked from risky sleep,
He stood before my bed,
And held a pistol in his hand,
Directed toward my head.

I sprang and seized him by the throat—
"You murderous thief," I cry,
"Your life—not mine—is forfeited—
You are the one to die!"

I held him in my rightful grasp,
He struggled for release;

"Don't shoot," he cried, "give me the spoils,
And let us make a 'PEACE!'"

CALL 'EM NAMES, JEFF.

SAID Beauregard to Lee and Jeff:
"Those Yankee sons of thunder,
Will scatter us from right to left,
Or cause us to knock under,
Unless we find some other way,
Of meeting their advances;
We've made up faces now so long,
They do not mind our glances."

"Oh! true," said Jeff, "I know it well;
How shall we change our game, sir?"
"Oh! dear," said Lee, "I cannot tell."
Quoth Beau, "We'll call 'em names, sir."
"That's good!" said Jeff; "you've hit it, Beau!"
Cried Lee: "That's what's the matter!
We'll call them Abolitionist,
And then you'll see them scatter!"

They rubbed their traitor hands in glee,
And issued stringent orders,
Signed by the polite Beauregard,
That henceforth, throughout their borders,
The only word that should be used
To name the Yankee soldier,
Should be an "Abolitionist!"
And then he strutted bolder.

They really thought that calling names
Had strengthened their position,
When all their sneaking curs up North
Run yelping "Abolition!"
But soon we made the traitors know
'Twas something else the matter;
The more they "Abolition" howled,
The more we didn't scatter.

We take the name you gave us, Beau.,
We mean to make it true, sir;
We'll first abolish slavery,
And then abolish you, sir!
You thought we'd guard your niggers, Jeff,
And keep them raising corn, sir,
To feed the traitor hordes you lead—
We'll do it in a horn, sir!

We'll free your blacks and fight your whites,
And dig for traitors graves, sir,
Until there's not in all the land
A traitor or a slave, sir!
When that is done, we'll home return—
(The homes to us so dear, sir,)
And soundly kick and cuff the curs
Now barking in our rear, sir!

BELMONT.

ULYSSES S. GRANT.

BY GEORGE W. BIRDSEYE.

GIVE us your hand, General Grant,
You're a man!
You were not the coward to say "I can't,"
Nor the boaster to say "I can!"
But you went to work with a will, and won,
To prove that the thing could be done.
Oh! God was kind, and heaven was true
When it gave us a man like U-
lysses Grant,
When it gave us a man like you!

We honor you, General Grant!
  You have made
The hearts of the nation with joy to pant,
  That were lying cold in the shade;
And they bless you ever for what you've done—
  For the glorious victories won,
  And pray that kind heaven may *grant* a few
  More such brave fighting men as U-
                lysses Grant,
  More such brave fighting men as you!

A PICTURE.

BY GEORGE W. BUNGAY.

WHEN the sweet roses, blushing red,
  In Eden their first fragrance shed,
A traitor and a copperhead
    Came in disguise,
Diffusing knowledge; and he said:
    "Eat and be wise,
And wisdom shall anoint thine eyes."

And when the woman saw the tree,
So pleasant for the eye to see,

She ate forbidden fruit. Thus she
        Hath men misled
Now 'neath the tree of Liberty
        This copperhead
Appears in blue and white and red.

Under the silent grass he hides,
Among the weeds and flowers he glides,
Down by the brooks he most abides—
        A treacherous thing;
The Stars and Stripes that deck his sides
        Conceal a sting;
Venom and death are in his spring.

Satan seceded, and he fell,
In chains and darkness doomed to dwell
With other traitors who rebel,
        In act and word,
Because he'd rather reign in hell
        Than serve the Lord,
Who guards us with his flaming sword.

AM I FOR PEACE?—YES!

BY DANIEL S. DICKINSON.

FOR the peace which rings out from the cannon's throat,
And the suasion of shot and shell,
Till rebellion's spirit is trampled down
To the depths of its kindred hell.

For the peace which shall follow the squadron's tramp,
Where the brazen trumpets bray,
And, drunk with the fury of storm and strife,
The blood-red chargers neigh.

For the peace that shall wash out the leprous stain
Of our slavery—foul and grim;
And shall sunder the fetters which creak and clank
On the down-trodden dark man's limb.

I will curse him as traitor, and false of heart,
Who would shrink from the conflict now;
And will stamp it, with blistering, burning brand,
On his hideous Cain-like brow.

Out! out of the way! with your spurious peace,
  Which would make us rebellion's slaves;
We will rescue our land from the traitorous grasp,
  Or cover it over with graves.

Out! out of the way! with your knavish schemes,
  You trembling and trading pack!
Crouch away in the dark, like a sneaking hound,
  That its master has beaten back.

You would barter the fruit of our fathers' blood,
  And sell out the Stripes and Stars,
To purchase a place with rebellion's votes,
  Or escape from rebellion's scars.

By the widow's wail, by the mother's tears,
  By the orphans who cry for bread,
By our sons who fell, we will never yield
  Till rebellion's soul is dead.

LAY OF THE MODERN "KONSERVATIVS."

BY CHARITY GRIMES.

I AM a gay "Konservativ,"
  I stand by the old Konstitution, I du;
 I go for the Union ez it was,
  With the old Dimmycrat ticket, rite thru.
These Black Republikans don't suit me,
Fur I'm a Konservativ man, yu see!

I am a Dimmycrat, dyed in the wool;
  I go fur free trade, and that sort ov thing;
I think it's rite tu let slavery rule—
  Sooner'n hev Lincoln, I'd vote fur a king,
And hev the Saouth fur an aristockracy,
To rule the hull North, (except the Dimmockracy.)

Shuttin' up folks fur speekin' their mind,
  In my opinion's a piece of knavery—
I go fur free speech ov every kind,
  Except when it interferes with slavery!
(Sich kind ov free speech all Dimmykrats fight--
Ef Brooks hed *killed* Sumner, he'd done jest right.)

I go fur aour konstitush'nal rights,
  With the rite ov *habeas corpus* invi'late;
I'll show 'em haow a Dimmykrat fights,
  Ef Abram Lincoln attempts tu spile it!
I've a right to *tawk* treason, ez I understand—
Tawk's tawk; it's *money* that buys the land!

I go for the vigorous conduct ov war,
  (Of course with a decent regard tu figgers,
So ez not tu inkreese aour national debt,)
  And abuv all *not* to free the niggers.
I'd ruther the North hed not pulled a trigger,
Than see a traitor shot down by a nigger.

Yes, I am a real Konservativ;
  I stand by the Konstitushun, I du!
Ef enny wun sez I'm frends with the Saouth,
  I'll sware by hokey it isn't true!
I *an't* a rebel; but, he—m!—*speak low*—
I *kinder* beleeve in Vallandigham, though!

ODE TO OLD ABE.

LET traitors rave and tories whine,
Stick to it Abraham, don't resign;
Your cause is just, the people true,
Let rebels growl, but put them through,
And you shall have the glory.

The people called you to the chair,
And legally they placed you there;
They don't regret the choice they made,
Nor will they fail to give you aid,
And you shall have the glory.

In guiding safe the ship of State,
Cares you have and trials great;
Beset you are on every side,
Do what you will you are belied,
But you shall have the glory.

If Breckinridge had carried the day,
There'd be no war his followers say;
No war of course could be maintained,
'Gainst cruel knaves, with freedom chained,
But Abraham spoiled his glory.

Four years more to mature his plans,
To chain our feet and tie our hands,
Four years more to plot and revel,
And send us headlong to the devil,
And Abe upset his glory.

Though many a brave and valiant son
Must die before our warring's done,
Our fathers' land shall yet be free;
Away with chains and slavery,
And Abe shall have the glory.

Let those who're rebels in disguise,
Go down with Jeff and sympathize;
If they want niggers, let them go
To Dixie's land where niggers grow,
And Abe shall have the glory.

In 'seventy-six our fathers saw
Just such tories hung by law;
In 'sixty-three their children see
Many unhung, who ought to be,
And Abe shall have the glory.

BURN YOUR COTTON.*

BY DR. S. SILSBEE.

BURN your cotton—burn it, burn it—
  Let the flaming incense rise,
With the shrieks of human chattels,
  'Mid the tortured "nigger's" cries.
Burn it, burn it! 'tis the emblem
  Of your infamy and pride;
Fitting offering on the altars
  Where man's freedom is denied.

Burn your cotton—oh! 'tis noble!
  Sweep the Mississippi's vale;
Ruin falls so cheap and easy
  On—who never owned a bale.
Oh! by all means burn the cotton,
  It is written—late or soon,
To whom gods have given madness
  "Hari Kari" is a boon.

Burn it, burn it, for the cotton
  Is the only thing you own;
Save the "niggers" and plantations,
  Where the fleecy staple's grown;

* See page 187, REBEL RHYMES.

All the rest is yours by pillage,
  And the pirate's law of might,
Yet you deprecate oppression,
  And pretend to prate of right.

Yes, by all means, burn your cotton,
  We will bear its loss as well
As the blind and foolish planters,
  Who but sing their final knell;
Shout the battle-cry of cotton,
  Light the fires, explode the mine;
Freedom never more will worship
  At your cotton monarch's shrine.

Burn your cotton, crazy traitors;
  'Tis your cue, without a doubt—
In the coming retribution
  You'll be nearly all "played out."
Burn your cotton, if it please you,
  For its blaze will furnish light
To the legions of the Union,
  Who are gathering in their might.

Burn your cotton, for the freemen
  Of the world are looking on;
When its fires fade, the footsteps
  Of the tyrants shall be gone.

Light it, light it! 'tis the battle
Torch of freedom and the brave,
To illuminate the Union
That our patriot fathers gave.

Fire your hearts, and burn the cotton—
Let the flames rise high and higher,
Till the last torch of rebellion
In the ashes shall expire.
And upon the blazing pyre, too,
Human slavery we'll fling,
Until justice—human justice—
And not Cotton, shall be King.

Cincinnati, August 10, 1862.

MY MARYLAND.

THE rebel feet are on our shore,
Maryland! My Maryland!
I smell 'em half a mile or more,
Maryland! My Maryland!
Their shockless hordes are at my door,
Their drunken generals on my floor,
What now can sweeten Baltimore?
Maryland! My Maryland!

Hark to our noses' dire appeal,
  Maryland! My Maryland
O unwashed rebs! to you we kneel,
  Maryland! My Maryland!
If you can't purchase soap, oh! steal
That precious article—I feel
Like scratching from the head to heel,
  Maryland! My Maryland!

You're covered thick with mud and dust,
  Maryland! My Maryland!
As though you'd been upon a bust,
  Maryland! My Maryland!
Remember, it is scarcely just,
To have a filthy fellow thrust
Before us, till he's been scrubbed fust,
  Maryland! My Maryland!

I see no blush upon thy cheek,
  Maryland! My Maryland!
It's not been washed for many a week,
  Maryland! My Maryland!
To get thee clean—'tis truth I speak—
Would dirty every stream and creek
From Potomac to Chesapeake,
  Maryland! My Maryland!

July, 1862.

TAKE NO STEP BACKWARD!

Inscribed to the Thirty-eighth Congress of the United States.

BY W. D. GALLAGHER.

TAKE no step backward! The eternal ages
Look down upon you from their height sublime,
And witness the events which history's pages
Shall class among the noblest of all time.
Right onward now the path of duty lieth,
Though it may lead to dangers that appal:
"Right onward! onward!" Justice sternly crieth,
And Mercy joins with Justice in the call.

Take no step backward! Centuries of oppression
Are culminating 'midst our nation's throes
And wrong that might have stood, with fair concession,
Yields to the force of self-inflicted blows.
The hand grown horny in the life-long labor
That clothed and pampered those who held it bound,
Now grasps the gun, or wields the flashing sabre,
And wins and wears its honors on the ground.

Take no step backward! Contraband or chattel,
Or slave or "person," what you will—*they're men!*
And if *we* stand or fall in this dread battle,
God leads the bondman from his thrall again.
The pillar of a cloud by day is hazing
The atmosphere where'er the battle lies:
The pillar of a fire by night is blazing
Where conflagration paints yon Southern skies.

Take no step backward! Ye have sorely smitten,
At hip and thigh the evil and the wrong;
What ye have said, now verify! what written,
Seal with the seal of action, broad and strong
Be not alarmed at apparitions dire
Of flaming swords that hurtle into view:
The element that purifies is fire:
Pass firmly on and resolutely through.

Take no step backward! Ye whom God now uses
To solve the problems of man's destiny,
To rectify his wrongs, right his abuses,
The grand accomplishment ye may not see:
But in the future—in the years of glory
That peace restored shall bring our land again—
Your names shall glitter in the noblest story
That celebrates the deeds of noblest men.

www.ingramcontent.com/pod-product-compliance
Lightning Source LLC
La Vergne TN
LVHW020127110826
845151LV00001B/300

* 9 7 8 1 4 2 5 5 4 0 2 9 6 *